Horst Bielfeld

Mice

Everything about Care, Nutrition, Diseases, Behavior, and Breeding

With 33 Color Photographs and 30 Drawings

Consulting Editor: Dr. Matthew M. Vriends, Ph.D.

BARRON'S

First English language edition published in 1985
by Barron's Educational Series, Inc.
© 1984 by Gräfe and Unzer GmbH, Munich,
West Germany.

The title of the German book is *Mäuse*

Translated by Maria Cooper, PhD

All inquiries should be addressed to:
Barron's Educational Series, Inc.
250 Wireless Boulevard
Hauppauge, NY 11788

International Standard Book No. 0-8120-2921-6

Library of Congress Catalog Card No. 84-23278
Library of Congress Cataloging in Publication Data
Bielfeld, Horst.
    Mice: everything about care, nutrition, diseases,
behavior, and breeding.

    Translation of: Mäuse.
    Includes index.
    1. Mice as pets.   I. Title.
SF459.M5B5413   1985   636'.93233   84-23278
ISBN 0-8120-2921-6

PRINTED IN HONG KONG
12 490 98

Front cover: Brown colored mouse and white mouse
    (albino mouse)
Inside front cover: Colored Siamese mouse
Inside back cover: Albino mice at play
Back cover: (top left) White mouse
    (top right) Colored mouse
    (bottom left) Harvest mouse
    (bottom right) Yellow-necked mouse

Photo credits:

Aichhorn: page 56 (bottom left, bottom right)
Bielfeld: inside front cover, page 45, back cover (top
    right)
Coleman/Burton: page 28, inside back cover
Coleman/Taylor: page 55 (bottom left)
Layer: pages 45 (top left, top right), 56 (top left, top
    right), back cover (bottom left)
Limbrunner: pages 45 (bottom), 55 (top, bottom
    right)
NHPA/Dalton: page 10 (top left, bottom right)
NHPA/Leach: page 56 (center left)
Reinhard: front cover, page 10 (bottom left)
Rogl: page 56 (center right), back cover (bottom
    right)
Wothe: pages 9, 10 (bottom right), 27 (top,
    bottom), back cover (top left)

Note of Warning

    This book deals with the keeping and care of mice as
pets. In working with these animals, you may occasionally sustain minor scratches or bites. Have such wounds
treated by a doctor at once.

    As a result of unhygienic living conditions, mice can
have mites and other external parasites, some of which
can be transmitted to humans or to pet animals, including
cats and dogs. Have infested mice treated by a veterinarian, if necessary (see page 42), and go to the doctor
yourself at the slightest suspicion that you may be harbor-
ing one of these pests. When buying mice, be sure to look
for the signs of parasite infestation (see page 17).

    Mice must be watched very carefully during the
exercise period in the house (see page 36). To avoid life-
threatening accidents, be particularly careful that your
pets do not gnaw on any electrical wires.

Contents

3

Contents

A Word of Introduction

It is not without reason that the mouse, persecuted by humans for centuries as an unwelcome rival for food, has also been treated with reverence, has even been celebrated as a hero—from the legends and sagas of classical antiquity to the cartoon characters of Tom and Jerry and Walt Disney's Mickey Mouse. The reason? More than any other animal, that adaptable little rodent is a master in the art of survival.

This "how to" book is concerned mainly with keeping and caring for white and colored mice—the domesticated descendents of the gray house mouse. Horst Bielfeld, an expert on small mammals and an experienced breeder of pet mice, describes how to care for white or colored mice, simulating their natural environment. Though domesticated mice usually are more gentle than their wild relatives and are not as shy, they have kept much of their original behavior, a fact any would-be keeper of these animals should not forget. There is nothing more entertaining for a mouse owner than to watch these quick and agile pets scrambling over their "condominium" or scurrying through their cage. This agility, alertness, and curiosity of mice, as well as their partiality to delicacies of all kinds, are their most striking behavioral characteristics.

Among the mammals, a mouse is outstanding for adaptability and love for play. The author explains how you can take advantage of the natural abilities of mice to hand-tame them quickly and to train them to perform little tricks.

It is very rare for mice to develop serious diseases, providing they are suitably housed and kept. Just in case, though, you'll find a comprehensive chapter containing descriptions of the major diseases mice are known to contract, and including a guide to diagnosis and treatment, and, even more important, disease prevention.

Many owners of mice like to observe the family life of their pets—watch their birth and their growing up. If you are interested in breeding pet mice, you'll find the necessary guidelines in this book. Hobby breeders find out how to pair the animals in order to breed any of the many varieties of color or fur type possible today. Some basic facts of mice genetics, written in clear and understandable English, provide the basic knowledge necessary for such breeding.

Finally, the special chapter "Understanding Mice," reviews the wild relatives of the colored pet mouse their fascinating community and social behavior patterns and their interaction with other mice or with predators.

Attractive color photographs and informative illustrations supplement the text. The author does not limit advice on successful breeding and keeping of mice to "how-to" instructions, but includes the reasons behind the recommendations. After a perusal of this book, even persons who have been prejudiced against mice will feel something akin to admiration for these tiny champions at survival. Readers will understand why mice are so successful in holding their own in nature, and why they have even been successful in capturing a place among the general public's favorite pets.

From Wild Animal to Pet

The Family of Mice

Mice belong to the order of rodents (Rodentia), by far the most numerous of all mammal orders with more than 300 genera numbering approximately 3,000 different species. Nearly one half of all the known mammals are rodents. The most prominent common characteristics of rodents are the two pairs of chisel-like, self-sharpening incisors (cutting or gnawing front teeth) that grow continuously. Canine teeth are lacking.

The smallest rodent in the world is the African harvest, or dwarf, mouse (*Mus minutoides*), a close relative of the house mouse. It is no more than 2 inches (5 centimeters), and it weighs less than ⅕ ounce (5–6 grams). The largest rodent, on the other hand, is South America's capybara or "water pig," which grows to more than 48 inches (1.2 meters), and weighs over 100 pounds (45 kilograms). Rodents prevail in almost all environments and climate zones—from the polar regions (lemming) to deserts (jumping mouse), from swamps and rivers (coypu, beaver) to the highest mountain peaks (chinchilla, pika), and from jungles (flame squirrel) to metropolitan areas (house mouse, house rat, brown rat). Some rodents live only underground (mole), others on trees (tree squirrel), and some have even learned to glide through the air (flying squirrel).

The mice family (Muridae) is not only the most numerous family of rodents—it has about 500 species—but also the largest family of the whole mammal class. Mice come in all shapes and sizes—tiny ones and large ones, some with long tails, some with big ears. All mice, however, have a pointed nose and a split upper lip. The long tail is practically hairless, with clearly visible scale rings. A mouse's forefeet have four toes each, the hindfeet have five. Originally, mice were limited to the Old World and to Australia. Humans themselves introduced mice, particularly the best known representatives of the family—the house mouse, black rat, and brown rat—to North America and to all the ends of the earth previously not populated by mice. That introduction, however, was usually involuntary and unwelcome (mostly as stowaways on ships, or in luggage or freight).

Compared to the history of the earth, that of the family of mice is relatively brief. It is believed that mice evolved from burrowing animals or rooters (family of Cricetidae) at the end of the Miocene Epoch (in the middle of the Tertiary Period, about 10 to 15 million years ago). Golden hamsters, the North American deer mice, or white-footed mice, jumping mice, and pocket mice, to name just a few, all belong to the rooters. Mice and rats of the family Muridae—in particular, the house mouse, the black house rat, and the brown rat—are the most "successful" of all mammals: they multiply extremely fast and are able to adapt to almost any environmental condition. No other mammal family has this ability to quite the same degree.

From Wild Animal to Pet

Many ancient peoples treasured mice as lucky charms or sacred animals. Here is a coin of the Hellenistic Period featuring a mouse.

The House Mouse in History

The house mouse has become an inseparable part of human history. Originally a wild field animal, the mouse probably attached itself to humans about 8,000 years ago, at the time when humans started to settle, turning from hunter to farmer and learning to grow and store grain. The mouse found very quickly that it was much easier to live on human stores, and that the presence of people meant safety from enemies. Yes, people soon enlisted the help of cats to exterminate the mouse—but never successfully! The adaptability of mice and their ability to multiply secured them a place not only in the annals of nature but also in human cultural history. The mouse was so indestructible and omnipresent that it became both a terrible pest and a myth.

The ancient Egyptians and Romans had an idiom that described the mouse's reproductive ability. They used to say, "it's raining mice," or, "mice are made of raindrops." Other people of the ancient world such as the Greeks and the people of India believed that mice were lightning bolts born of thunderstorms or other thunderous beings approaching in black clouds, darting their lightning spears down to earth. Mice were seen either as a plague sent by God or as an instrument of punishment. At any rate, people would present sacrificial offerings either to stop a mouse plague or to prevent one; mice were also kept in temples and worshiped as sacred animals.

More than 4,000 years ago, the Cretans built a temple in Tenedos, Pontus, where they fed and worshiped mice. In the Cretan victory over Pontus, according to legend, mice helped by chewing through the leather straps of the shields of the Pontic soldiers so that they were unable to defend themselves.

Paintings on ancient bowls and other clay artifacts tell us that the Egyptians were also keeping mice about 4,000 years ago. It is believed that the first white and spotted mice appeared about that time in Greece and Egypt as well as in China. White mice in particular were considered sacred. People kept them in their temples or homes and used them to predict the future, or as lucky charms, or to keep the wild mice away. Waltzing mice originated in China; they have been known there for 2,000 to 3,000 years. More than 300 years ago, the Japanese started to breed white and colored mice systematically. From there, the first of these special mice were introduced into Europe and North America about 150 years ago.

In ancient Rome and during the Middle Ages, mice were used as medicine against all kinds of diseases. They were dried, pulverized, sliced, or marinated in oil, and then used either as a compress to be put on wounds or ailing body parts, or taken orally. Even the blood of mice was a favored ingredient of drugs and tonics. It is hard to believe what mice, in various forms, were supposedly good for; flesh wounds, snakebites, warts, bladder irregularities, diabetes, enlarged thyroid glands, diseases of the eye, and loss of hair were just a few of the ailments that mice were allegedly able to heal. Even though it is known that people used mice for medicinal purposes, all kinds of means—excluding the cat—were recommended to get rid of these same mice. The cat, natural enemy of the mouse, did not have an easy life during the Middle Ages. Hated as an accomplice of sorcerers and witches, it suffered the same cruel treatment as the women who were branded as witches. People just did not recognize the cat as their friend and as a mouse exterminator.

The House Mouse Today

Walt Disney's comic strips and cartoons of Mickey Mouse might well be considered a modern-day myth. Since his "birth" in 1928, Mickey Mouse has been on a triumphant victory march around the world. In Disney's own words, Mickey represents the clever, tiny mouse hunted by everybody. But thanks to his special skills, he always just barely triumphs, no matter how treacherous the situation. In all those cartoons, Mickey survives his adventures by the same clever means the house mouse has to employ each and every day to survive—even though its struggles are certainly not always amusing.

Without doubt, Mickey Mouse is the most famous mouse in the world today. The stories have been translated into many languages, adapting our hero's name to Micky, Mikke, or Miki, all sounding like "Mickey." In Italian, Mickey became "Topolino"; in Japanese and Arabic, even the characters representing his name look like the tracks of a mouse. Mickey and all the other "fairy tale mice" are secure from deadly persecution; their living model, on the other hand, the house mouse, is constantly hounded with poison and traps. Actually, humans are indebted particularly to the white mice serving as laboratory mice, for they have played an important role in researching countless diseases and pharmaceuticals. A lover of mice will understand and support the value of mice and know and appreciate white as well as colored mice as the lovable and interesting pets they are.

White mouse and dark brown mouse drinking from a water dispenser.

From Wild Animal to Pet

The White Mouse (Albino Mouse)

At present, the colored mouse is the favorite pet mouse, but until recently, the favorite was the white mouse. At least that is the animal's common name; experts call it the albino mouse, a variety not to be confused with the so-called self white mouse, which fanciers sub-divide into Pink-eyed (P.E. white) and Black-eyed (B.E. white) varieties (see color photo on page 45).

Mouse meets mouse: The animals sniff at each other's head.

The albino mouse has the typical albino characteristics: red eyes and snow-white fur without any pigmentation; the mouse, therefore, looks pure white. This phenomenon, called albinism, is the result of a mutation—a sudden unpredictable change in a hereditary factor (a gene or its carrier chromosome). As you can see from the historic examples (see page 7), there must have been quite a few albinos among the wild mice of ancient times.

By careful breeding over many years, today's pet white mice are much more gentle and less timid than their ancestors, the wild house mice. But they have retained the ancestral behavioral characteristics, and that is why they are so much fun to watch and to handle.

Some genes of these albino mice may still carry latent color factors that are handed down recessively and are invisible. There may be factors for yellow, for the natural mouse color, or for black, brown, or many other colors. Only pairing a white and a colored mouse and examining the offspring will reveal the presence of any undisclosed color factors in the albino mouse. The albino is, therefore, a very interesting partner in the breeding of colored mice (see page 54).

The different strains of white laboratory mice, on the other hand, are bred as pure as possible; most of them are inbred strains with definite characteristics and known genetic makeup. They even have their own names: One of the better known American laboratory albinos belongs to a strain called BALB.

Feeding mice.
Top left and bottom right: wild house mouse; top right and bottom left: white mouse (albino mouse).

From Wild Animal to Pet

The size and weight of white mice vary with individual strains; in general, they are a bit larger and heavier than the wild house mouse. Some animals may grow to a length of 8.5 inches (22 centimeters) and weigh over 2 ounces (56 grams). The nature of mice being what it is, pet mice can provide joy and entertainment for all of their short life; and white mice are just as suited for that as colored ones.

Colored Mice

The first colored mice, like the first white mice, evolved long before recorded time (see **page 11**); we know that there were a black mouse and a black mouse with a white belly in ancient times; other color combinations are more recent. Selective breeding—that is, breeding for specific traits such as specific color combinations—has been possible only since the basic principles of genetics were discovered. Early color mutations almost always disappeared because people had no idea how to pair the animals to make the new color appear in the offspring and become hereditary through generations. Once this hurdle had cleared, a breeding euphoria set in. It did not just include mice, but all kinds of pets—lovebirds, canaries, zebra finches, even the guinea pig. All of these animals produced a variety of colors, the mouse most of all.

With mice, successive generations are born so fast that breeders were able to determine the effects of certain mutations very quickly, learning which color combi-nations were possible. Hobby breeders as well as scientists bred a large number of colors and color combinations (see color photos on **page 46**). Here are just a few examples: natural color, natural color with a white belly, yellow, black, black with yellow belly, blue, blue-green, silver, silver-cinnamon, silver-fawn-brown, brown, cinnamon brown, light cinnamon yellow, fawn, light fawn-colored, cafe au lait, chocolate brown, seal brown, sable brown, cream-colored, red, black tans, chocolate tan, cinnamon tan, pearl tan, and many marked varieties, such as Dutch, brokens, rump white, and Himalayans. Breeders have given some of the more re-cent strains such flowery names as Dove, Silver Fox, Pearl, Seal Point Siamese, and Argente.

This list of colors and color combina-tions, which is by no means complete, shows the phenomenal variety possible. Most of these mice are not homozygotic (purebred); that is, the mice have genes for a number of different colors. Only pairing will show what surprises they might be hiding. There are, however, purebred

A mouse skillfully uses its forefeet for feeding.

micc. There are black ones, for instance (see color photo on page 27), and the tiny creatures of an inbred strain called C57B1 have become famous laboratory mice. Most of the colored mice are treasured by mice lovers who enjoy the pretty color variations. Owners try to increase the already impressive color scale by random breeding or by using expertise in selective breeding.

Waltzing Mice

Waltzing, or dancing, mice, mutants of the Wagnerian House Mouse (see page 61), are almost always spotted black and white (Dutch marked), often showing one white spot on their back, a white blaze on their face, and a white belly. They are dwarfish; their development is already stunted in the nest, and you can clearly distinguish them from their more normal brothers and sisters after about one week. When approximately 16 days old, the mice are deaf from a severely damaged middle ear, which disturbs their sense of balance. In addition, a defective pituitary gland (hypophysis) causes growth retardation. Waltzing mice, therefore, are rather weak, and stop growing after about 14 days. Because of their defects, they can neither jump nor climb, and some, depending on the degree of damage, are unable to walk in a straight line. Instead, they spin around in circles, especially early in the morning and at night. In this so-called "waltzing," they stagger and spin from very slowly to very fast, with uncontrolled head movements. Because of their loss of balance,

they cannot swim. They are delicate animals with little resistance; it is not surprising, therefore, that they are not very prolific. The young of a pair of waltzing mice are unable to survive. If you want to have waltzing mice, you have to pair a normal mouse with "dancing genes" and a waltzing mouse. In this breeding example, there is the theoretical chance that 50% of the litter will be waltzers. Since waltzing mice have severe defects, not many grow to maturity; they die early or are even born dead. An animal lover who knows that waltzing mice are brain-damaged will find it hard to enjoy their waltzing and will probably not want to keep them.

Preliminary Considerations

Is a Mouse Right for You?

Every pet—even a tiny one like a mouse—changes the daily routine of its keeper, and usually that of the family. If you are thinking of getting a mouse, or mice, all family members should discuss this desire and whether each family member would make a good and persevering mouse keeper. It is certainly not very difficult to take care of a tiny mouse, or even several mice, but it is still a good idea to consider exactly what kind of responsibilities you will be undertaking.

There are no great problems involved in keeping mice. That is just why those small duties, performed with enthusiasm at first, can easily be underestimated and all too soon become drudgery. The following little test is designed to help you find out whether you would make a good pet keeper.
• Does every member of the family agree to the purchase of a mouse (several mice)?
• Is everybody free of prejudice against mice? (Disgust, nausea?)
• Will everyone hold the mice without reluctance?
• Is everyone ready to take care of the animals as long as they live—for example, if the actual owner is on vacation?
• Are you prepared to buy a suitable cage for your mice, of sufficient size, complete with exercise wheel and the best accessories?
• Do you have at least an hour a day to play with your mice and to take care of them?
• If your mice should become ill, will you take them to a vet and, if necessary, pay for expensive medication?
• Will you care for a sick mouse, even if it means cleaning it of urine, diarrheic droppings, or pus? Would you give up a weekend trip to care for your sick pet?
• Are you able to give up smoking for the sake of the health of your mice, or at least abstain from smoking in the room where the animals are kept?

If you can honestly say ''yes'' to all these questions, then a mouse is in good hands with you.

Children and Mice

Mice are not toys for small children. A mouse is too tiny and delicate to be petted or held by a toddler. A toddler is still unable to control the pressure of his hands sufficiently to avoid hurting the little creatures. A guinea pig is different; it takes the rough handling without complaining and without fighting back; a mouse, on the other hand, would bite immediately.

By the time children reach school age, when they are five or six, they are quite ready to take care of mice, pick them up correctly, and hold them in their hand. Naturally, someone has to show them how to do this—either the parents, the pet shop owner, or the breeder selling the animal. Parents inexperienced in handling mice might as well listen too. This is very important because there will be times when the child is unwilling or unable to look after the well-being of his or her pet (because of illness, school trips, occasional disinterest). It is important that parents or brothers and sisters be able to take over during those times, without immediately putting pressure on a neglectful child, particularly with the unfortunate threat, "You take care of this thing, or I'll get rid of it!" Such situations need loving intuition; if the parents talk to their child about their own experiences with the animals, parents may well rekindle lost interest. A child loves his mouse, even if, at times, it doesn't look that way. Suddenly "getting rid" of an animal can cause severe grief in a child, not to mention the loss of trust in parents.

Do You Want a Male or Female?

If you want to keep only a single mouse, it doesn't matter whether you choose a male or female, though you might prefer a female because of its more gentle nature. A female also does not produce as much mousy odor. But with just one mouse and regular cage cleaning, odor should not be a problem.

You recognize adult males by the clearly visible scrotum on the base of the tail (left). In a female (right), the anal and genital body openings are closer together. In young females whose skin is not yet furry, you can see the nipples.

A male mouse shows a bit more temperament and is usually a somewhat faster learner when it comes to little tricks. On the other hand, its inclination to leave scent-marks everywhere is a less agreeable trait. Contrary to popular opinion, male mice are not quicker to bite, nor do they bite more fiercely; both sexes will bite when they feel threatened or are picked up awkwardly.

Determining the Sex of Mice

With adult mice, it is really not difficult to distinguish between male and female. Without having to pick up the animals, you can recognize males by the oblong thickening at the base of the tail. This is the elongated scrotum that protrudes beyond the anal opening. The skin is hairy, just as the reat of the body. The distance between anal and genital openings is almost twice that of the female mouse. A male's genital opening is round, and light pressure on the mouse's belly causes the penis to emerge, at least partially (see foregoing illustration).

It is a little more difficult to distinguish male from female in young mice of three or four weeks. The distance between their body openings has not yet developed fully. But sexing is still possible. If you pull the skin of a mouse's rear underside towards the front with your thumb and index finger, a male's testicles will descend into the scrotum.

The sex of mice two to three weeks old cannot be determined by their genitals, at least not with certainty. However, sexing is quite a bit easier at the age of 8 to 11 days, when a mouse's belly does not yet have hair. In a female mouse at that age, the ten nipples are clearly visible, arranged in two rows on the stomach area.

Are Two Mice Happier?

In their natural state, mice share their burrows with their family or colony (see page 66). Therefore, the question of whether two mice are happier than one can only be answered by an emphatic "yes." Two mice can do all those things to each other that a person, as a mouse's substitute partner, is unable to do. The mice groom and lick each other in all the places they cannot reach themselves. They keep each other warm, and they converse by means of odor and body language (see pages 71 and 72).

Two mice should certainly be considered when you do not have sufficient time to give to a single pet. No fear, the animals will not become timid with you because they have each other's company, unless, of course, they don't get any attention from you beyond their food and drink. If you get two young mice and play with them regularly, they will become very tame and remain tame as long as they live.

If you decide on two mice—and want to stick to that number—besure you are getting two males, or two females! There is no clear answer to the question of whether two males or two females are easier on a mouse keeper (see page 15). Two males might be somewhat more lively, but they also give you more of the mousy odor, and they may fight with each other. Most of the time, however, they get along just fine, because one becomes subordinate to the other. Females will get into an occasional fight, as well, but they make up quickly. They seem to be a little more docile than males.

Mice love to move and run about, so no cage should be without an exercise wheel.

Where to Buy Mice

Sometimes it isn't easy to obtain a white or a colored mouse. That is why I am including a few tips at this point about where you'll find mice for sale.

Your first stop would naturally be the pet shop. But you might be surprised at the number of small local pet shops not carrying mice. The reasons are many: One owner told me that all those mice were just too much work and too much mouse odor for him. Another owner said that food and bedding material usually cost more than the eventual sale of the animals would net. The result of my small-scale pet shop poll: Of ten stores, seven sold mice.

Pet sections of certain department stores also usually offer a good selection of mice. You'll at least be able to buy white mice there, sometimes colored ones. If you know someone in a medical research institute, you might be able to get a mouse there. These laboratories almost always have white mice; you might even get an occasional black one. Finally, there are more hobby breeders than you think; but you usually do not find them in the Yellow Pages or in newspaper ads. If you do know a breeder, buy your mouse from him or her. Then you can be sure—as with reputable pet shops—that you are getting a strong, healthy animal, and with luck, even in the color you prefer. Many hobby breeders are so fascinated by the variety of colors that they will breed the most extraordinary hues.

And then there are children—they will sometimes just come home with a tiny mouse, offspring of a friend's pair of mice, and, to the parents' surprise, all of a sudden, "there's a mouse in the house!"

How to Choose Mice

First of all, choose young, immature animals. Mice have a very short life span; they usually live only 1½ to 3½ (seldom 7) years. Young mice will get used to you and become tame much faster. Several younger mice will scuffle their way into a community structure rather quickly, while older ones might fight lengthy, bitter wars that can even end with the death of the losers.

You should examine the mice you are buying very carefully to be sure that none of them is diseased. Healthy mice have clear, alert eyes and are very mobile and slim. The fur color of young animals is more intense, more glossy than that of older ones; ears are more delicate and show a little more hair.

When choosing your mouse, watch for the following:
• The animal should be neither too fat nor too skinny; excess weight usually signifies that a mouse is more than a year old. Lumps or nodules under the skin also indicate an older animal.
• The fur should be without bald spots; loss of hair is almost always incurable, and the animals might be suffering from mites, lice, mange, or eczema.
• The back should not be arched, nor the fur shaggy; these conditions usually indicate the presence of an internal disease.
• The anal area should not be soiled (diarrhea).
• There should be no symptoms of severe disease, such as paralysis, inactive sitting with straddled legs, head carried at an angle, or spinning movements.

What About Your Mice and Your Vacation?

To take a mouse (or two) on a vacation should not present too many problems. A

Preliminary Considerations

small but practically arranged mouse cage is ideal for this purpose. If you do not have one yet, consider buying one; its purchase will come in handy. If you usually keep your mice in a large cage or a mouse condo, these extra small cages can serve as an excellent home away from home during cleaning time. The smallest mice or hamster cages are sufficient as vacation cages. Check the distance between wires or bars of hamster cages, though. Bars should not be more than about 7/16 inch (10 mm) apart; about 5/16 inch (7.5 mm) is better. Such a cage fits easily into a small box or bag, protecting the animals from drafts and too much light during a car, bus, or train trip. Otherwise, mice take traveling well. Just put sufficient food and some juicy fruit into their cage; water might spill and get the whole cage wet.

You can even take a cage with a mouse or two as hand luggage onto a plane, but it is always advisable to ask the airline before you get to the airport. For international flights, you should consult the consulate of the country to which you are traveling. Since you can expect problems on international trips to any country, with any animal, it is a good idea to board your mice if you are planning to go abroad.

Relatives, friends, or acquaintances usually won't mind taking care of your pets for a few days. Provide the friend with a list of chores, with sufficient food and litter, and with all other necessary equipment (replacement for food and drink containers in the event that one should break). This way, you save your vacation substitute additional work.

If none of your friends or relatives is available for mouse-sitting, there's always the pet shop, your veterinarian, or the humane society. Boarding will cost you a little; on the other hand, you won't have the expense of food and bedding during this period.

Your Mouse's Home

White mice are extremely adaptable, but even though they might accept almost any kind of accommodation, you should provide a sufficiently large and easily cleanable home for your mice—both for the health of the animals and for the comfort of your nose.

Choosing the Type of Home

I know of instances where children have kept mice in large jars and cans, even in cigar boxes and cartons. However, wood and cardboard will soak up mouse urine, making it almost impossible to remove it. The result is that mouse quarters of this kind become a rather smelly affair in a very short time. Cardboard boxes have the additional disadvantage that the mice might gnaw their way out of them. I once explained these problems to a little girl who promptly answered, "My mouse doesn't do that! And besides, she gets a new box every week; I can get those free at the supermarket." And her mouse did, in fact, seem to be very content. Naturally, a home conforming more to the nature of a mouse is better for the animals, as well as for their owners. There are several choices for good mouse homes. Among these are a barred cage, an aquarium, a terrarium, and a condo.

Model of a mouse cage for a small mouse colony, furnished with suitable accessories: exercise wheel, climbing poles, connecting planks, hiding places, nest box, bedding and gnawing materials. Naturally, a feeding dish and demand water bottle are also part of the interior decoration.

Your Mouse's Home

The Mouse Cage

Pet shops and pet departments of large stores do offer a good selection of mouse cages (see illustration). Just make sure that the cage is not too small. For a single mouse, or even a pair, a cage should be about 16 inches wide by 12 inches deep by about 9 inches high (40 × 30 × 23 centimeters). Because of the small size and slimness of the animals, the bars of the cages cannot be too far apart. The ideal distance is about 5/16 inch (7.5 millimeters). Cages of this kind are designed with a removable plastic bottom tray for easy and thorough cleaning and disinfection. Your cage also needs a wire roof—otherwise the mice will just climb out! These roofs are hinged so that you can easily reach every last corner of the cage and care for and play with your mice.

Don't choose a smaller cage; you want your animals to be able to run around freely and to explore a larger territory. Mice stay healthier and more active when they have a lot of room.

In contrast to an aquarium or terrarium, a barred cage has the advantage of providing the mice with a more balanced environmental climate; the air circulates more freely. The disadvantage: By burrowing and running, the mice may scatter litter and food particles, making a mess of the area immediately surrounding the cage.

Aquarium or Terrarium

An aquarium, particularly one made of Plexiglas, can also serve as an excellent home for your mice. Just be sure that it is not too deep; otherwise an insufficient air supply might make the animals sick. If you choose an aquarium of Plexiglas, you can drill a few small holes into the upper part of the narrow sides to improve ventilation.

A flat, transparent container (a terrarium) with a large floor area and low sides but at least 8 inches [20 centimeters] high does not have just the advantage of good air circulation; it also provides the mice with a small "race track," satisfying a mouse's need for movement. However, since young mice particularly are known for their high leaps and bounds, it is advisable to cover the container with a wire mesh frame. You can easily make such an escape-proof fitting yourself with a few pieces of wood and a piece of wire mesh.

I keep my mice in a box approximately 3 feet 3 inches by 1 foot 5 inches by 1 foot 1 inch (98 × 42 × 33 centimeters). The box is made of plastic and has a Plexiglas window along the front. The grill on top is

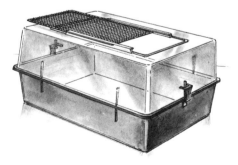

A terrarium can serve as a spacious and practical mouse house; the upper part made of Plexiglas is removable for easy cleaning.

provided with feeding doors. By means of a dividing wall or screen, the box can be partitioned into two separate cages.

The Mouse Condo

Mice love to run, to climb, to do gymnastics of all kinds—and they do a lot of it. Not only is this activity good for their health; it is also fun to watch. A mouse condominium, perhaps better termed a "pueblo" or, as the Germans call it, a "mouse citadel", is therefore a very appropriate and interesting way of housing your mice. White mice as well as colored mice are very cautious and will not dare jump a sizable vertical distance. You can thus keep your mice on such a condo without having to bother with wires or bars!

When building a condo, you can indulge your imagination; there are so many possibilities for design and "interior decoration." The basic model described here serves just to point out a few ground rules, to ensure that your mouse's dream house won't become a mousetrap, threatening the health or life of your pets. A small table with floor clearance of at least 20 inches (about 50 centimeters) makes a perfect base for your condo; normal table height is even better. The table top has to extend beyond the legs, however, so that it is impossible for the mice to get to the legs or to a pedestal; otherwise the legs will become a slide into freedom. Raising all the platform edges with a narrow strip of wood prevents food, bedding, nest material, feeding and drinking bowls, or toys from falling down. A board of pressed wood or

plastic with a surface of rough formica makes an ideal base; mice can really run on it without slipping, and such a board is easy to clean. For hygienic purposes, it is practical to use this same material to construct all the floors. These platforms have to be big enough so that you can connect them by tilted ladders or slides. Having completed the basic structure, you can furnish the platforms according to their use—sleeping, feeding, playing, exercising, and waste elimination.

Instead of a condo, you can also build a mouse apartment, like a dollhouse, with several "rooms" interconnected by slanting walkways and furnished with small furniture. It goes without saying that the

You can build your mouse condo on a table. This ideal way to keep mice affords the owner an exceptionally close, immediate view of the life style of his animals.

whole structure has to be very sturdy; each level must be fastened to the next one so that nothing can shake or fall over, injuring your mice or giving them the opportunity to run off. Wood pieces as supports, glued and screwed to the floor boards, will give your house stability. That stability is needed because mice, with all their gnawing and physical activity, can really "shake up" a place.

A mouse condo, suitable for one mouse or several mice, has obvious advantages. You will tend to spend more time with your pets; this, in turn, will make them so tame and playful that they'll lean far over the table edge in anticipation, ready to be entertained, whenever someone comes near.

Where to Put the Mouse's Home

A mouse cage—or other home—should be placed anywhere between table level to eye level. This is much better than putting the cage on the floor or on top of a high cabinet. Near the floor it is drafty and the animals do not get as much attention; they also scare easier when anyone approaches and will undoubtedly not become as tame as mice looking at you eye-to-eye. If they must live near the ceiling on top of some cabinet, they'll get noticed even less and they'll breathe stale warm air.

Accordingly, a mouse condo should be designed (see **page 21**) so that its upper platforms are at least at eye level. When choosing a location for your mouse house, avoid direct sunlight as much as dark corners. Mice prefer normal or slightly sub-

dued light. Also avoid placing a cage close to any heat sources. Like you, mice feel most comfortable in normal room temperature; a temperature of 64°F–68°F (18°C–20°C) is best for their health.

The Right Bedding

Sawdust or wood shavings make an excellent bedding material. They are available, cleaned and prepared, from your pet shop. Getting your shavings from a local carpenter or sawmill is not advisable. First, the shavings are very dusty; secondly, they might be contaminated by wild mice who place urine markers everywhere to identify their territory. Your mouse might contract a disease, and you would have no idea as to its origin.

To minimize odor many mouse owners put a layer of cat litter underneath the wood shavings, or at least into the corners of the cage. Others swear by natron (available as hydrated sodium carbonate in some drugstores, or in the form of baking soda). Pouring a little of the powder into the corners of the cage just about guarantees that it will be odor-free. Naturally, this does not mean that you can avoid regular cleaning; for reasons of hygiene, cleaning is very important (see **page 37**).

Lately, the market has been offering biological litter for small animals. It is relatively expensive but has excellent absorbent qualities and keeps a cage germ-free and odor-free. If the cost keeps you from using this bedding exclusively, try placing a little of it into the cage corners.

Your Mouse's Home

Mice are not quite as reliable as cats when it comes to choosing a "toilet" location, but they usually evacuate in the corners of a cage. Deodorizing the corners with litter or sodium carbonate will therefore minimize any annoying odor. But it is still a good idea to replace all the bedding material each time you clean the cage, since the mousy odor permeates all of it.

The Right Accessories

You are having a lot of fun with your pets, and you would like to keep it that way. That is why you should buy practical accessories. That includes a sturdy, easy-to-clean feeding dish and a water dispenser that won't drip or fall down. Reliable pet shops offer a variety of feeding and drinking utensils of demonstrated worth (see the illustration on page 25), but unfortunately, you'll also find much inadequate paraphernalia. Mice will turn over any food dish that is too light or unstable, scattering food all over the cage. They will chew through any bowl made of soft plastic. There are gravity-feed, demand-type water bottles that will not dispense a drop of water, no matter how hard the mice are sucking; others leak water. But clean food and drinking water are extremely important for the health of your mice!

Mice should have a small sleeping box in their cage. Certainly, they will build a nest of straw, hay, grass, cotton bedding, shredded paper, or strips of cloth, even if they do not have a sleeping box. But they are much more comfortable in their own little hiding place. Naturally, they'll haul all kinds of nesting material into their box; no cage should therefore be without it. Use only uncontaminated grass or hay—not easily found in today's metropolitan areas. Cleaned hay suitable for animals is available at most pet shops. Or you might grow your own little patch of grass in a flower pot on your window sill. Give your mice only unprinted paper; printing ink is damaging to animals.

You can place your mouse's sleeping quarters high in the cage, accessible by a ladder or tunnel. Your pet shop offers a good selection of suitable nesting houses, with or without stairs. Many amateurs will probably want to build this hideaway. There is no reason why you shouldn't be your own architect, but stay away from wood as building material; it picks up odor too easily. Mice will not soil their nest, but they do mark its boundaries with urine. Wood absorbs moisture, and with it the odor of the urine, which is extremely hard to remove. By the way, this applies not only to nest houses but also to your pets' toys, to ladders, teeter-totters, swings, and climbing devices. I recommend plastics for these accessories. Just don't forget to provide your mice with substitute gnawing material like small pieces of wood; they love birch or hazel twigs, for instance. If you do use wooden equipment, wash it in hot water and disinfect it regularly.

Since mice are vivacious creatures who need a lot of activity, an exercise wheel belongs in every mouse house. Some people might still see such a wheel as an instance of cruelty to animals, believing mice are chasing themselves to death. But they run on the wheel voluntarily and love every minute of it. Anyone who ever cared for a white or colored mouse will confirm this. Even mice with a lot of room to roam about (run of a room, large mouse condo), will regularly return to their wheel for some fitness training (see color photo on page 28).

There are plastic and metal exercise wheels, some freestanding, others screwed to the side of a cage. I prefer metal wheels, because the mice can't chew them up. Should you have a very noisy or squeaking wheel, a little oil or grease on the bearings will usually go a long way towards quiet exercise sessions.

Diet and Nutrition

Mice are moderate eaters, but, given the opportunity, will eat just about anything edible. They often prefer foods that are not meant for them and that do not agree with them—fatty foods like sausage, cheese, or oily seeds, for example. This kind of nourishment is actually bad for mice; it will make them too fat or even sick.

Wrong or unbalanced diets may cause a number of deficiencies, with devastating results for mice (see **page 38**).

Concentrated Feed

In their natural state, mice feed primarily on starch-filled seeds of all kinds, particularly grains, grass seed, millet, and rice. For that reason, the concentrated feed for your mice should be primarily grains.

Choose the best quality of grain mixture available at your pet shop, making sure that it consists mainly of the ingredients just listed. A small amount of oily seeds such as hemp or sunflower seeds does no harm, as long as the mice do not pick just those seeds out of a grain and seed mixture. In that case, you'd have to ration the concentrated feed, or at least the oily seeds.

Mice and mice keepers prefer the mixture of staple foods shown in the following table, or one of similar concentrations. It provides not only all the necessary nutrients but also a variety of flavors. For that reason, I, too, like this kind of feed, even if the mice might be finicky, leaving one or two of the seed or grain varieties untouched. If you are feeding a whole colony of mice, it will probably be more economical to mix the feed yourself. There is no harm in changing the composition if you should run out of some of the grain varieties.

Other highly nutritious foods belonging to this "bread and cereal group" are old whole grain bread, rolls, crackers, or plain white bread; the harder the bread the better the dental care it provides (see **page 44**). Don't forget to include these tidbits when calculating the total amount of concentrated feed for your pet mice.

Food bowls or racks have to be sturdy or should be fastened to the cage bars to keep them from tipping over. To prevent contamination, offer drinking water in a demand-type dispenser bottle.

Diet and Nutrition

Seed Concentrations

Proportions and nutritional values in %

	Amount in %	Fats	Carbohydrates	Proteins	Minerals
Wheat	10	2	70	10	2
Oats (husked)	20	5	58	11	3
Barley	5	2	68	9	2
Buckwheat	5	2	59	11	3
Corn (cracked)	10	4	70	9	1
Rice (natural)	10	2	63	8	5
Millet (La Plata)	15	3	59	13	3
Canary or white seed	10	6	52	15	6
Grass seed	10	2	55	6	2
Sunflower seeds (husked)	1	54	6	20	2
Hemp	1	30	20	23	2
Linseed	3	35	21	18	6

All-Purpose Mouse Food

If you are keeping large numbers of mice, you are usually advised to feed all-purpose mice food pellets. There is absolutely nothing wrong with that. These pellets contain the correct concentrations of all the nutrients, vitamins, minerals, and trace elements that mice need. But I know from experience with my own animals that mice keep changing their taste, preferring sometimes this, sometimes that. For that reason, I like to offer them as much variety in their diets as possible.

Greens and Fruits

In addition to grains and seeds, mice like a certain amount of greens and juicy fruits. They'll love it when you bring them some tender grass. They won't eat all of it but just nibble at the goodies, mouse-fashion. Other possible green vegetables are head lettuce and endive, brussels sprouts, dandelions, and shepherd's purse. Mice also like to munch on carrots, apples,

Fresh greens are important. Top: Black-colored mouse. Bottom: White mouse (albino mouse).

Diet and Nutrition

pears, grapes, cucumbers, or boiled potatoes, as well as other fruits, like raspberries and strawberries, raw and dried figs (particularly their seeds), dates, and raisins.

Greens and fruits are an important dietary supplement (see "Deficiency Diseases," page 38), but they have to be fresh, clean, and dry (see "The Correct Way to Feed Mice," page 31). There are some animals—birds, for instance, and even a few rodents—who can live without water, deriving all the liquid they need from the foods they eat. Your pet mouse, on the other hand, does need additional drinking water (see page 30).

Fodder

By coarse fodder for mice I mean good hay. A mouse won't eat very much of it, but if you give it a little hay as nesting material, it will certainly nibble on it. Good, clean hay is very aromatic; it should not be dusty or have a musty odor. Moldy or contaminated hay can damage the animals' health (see "The Right Bedding", page 22).

Animal Proteins

Primarily, a mouse's diet consists of starchy grains, a few oily seeds, and a little bit of meat and other animal proteins.

White mice in an exercise wheel.

Wild mice will occasionally grab a caterpillar, worm, or even an insect or a spider; they will not hunt insects, however. Nursing mothers, in particular, sometimes develop a craving for animal proteins that they need to increase their milk production. They will eat a bit of hamburger meat, a mealy worm, or a morsel of mild cheese right out of your hand, and you can see that they are enjoying their gourmet dinner. Or you might try a piece of cooked chicken, beef heart, or other lean meat. Do not feed them salty or spicy meat, however.

Your mouse's normal diet may also include a little hard-boiled egg yolk or some bacon. Both contain a high amount of fat but are very healthy for mice if given in moderation. There are breeders who buy chicken feed consisting mainly of grains, welcoming the shrimps contained in this feed as a dietary protein supplement for their mice. In fact, though mice find shrimp tempting, you should not feed them to your pet. Shrimp are extremely rich in proteins, and the mice would be getting too much of a good thing. In addition, your mice might contract salmonellosis, a dangerous infectious disease (see page 40.)

How Much Food?

For concentrated feed, this question is an easy one to answer: If you use a feeding dish or bowl, give your mouse approximately one level tablespoon (6 grams) in the morning and at night. Should you find the food gone within a relatively short time, with no leftovers scattered about the cage or hidden in "secret" corners, increase your rations to a heaping tablespoon (about 8–10 grams). Too much concentrated feed will cause a mouse to become too fat, a problem easily encountered when you are using a hopper or basket.

Healthy mice will usually not gorge themselves, but they will dig out large amounts of feed to rummage for their favorite tidbits, usually the seeds containing the most oil. In this process, they often spill more than half of their food into the bedding where it will be contaminated.

If you do like to use a hopper dispenser or basket, pellets are a preferable choice (see **page 26**). With this type of feed, your mouse does not really have a reason to take more food than needed, since all pellets are of equal size, look, and taste. But some mice will still not be satisfied until all of the food is out of the dispenser. Should you find yourself with one of these, your only choice is individual bowl feeding.

With a pellet dispenser, you normally do not have to limit the amount of food. The mice will take only what they need. However, the chosen type of dispenser should be small enough to prevent the food from becoming old and musty. A practical rule of thumb for buying the correct size: A hopper should hold about one week's food supply.

How about fresh greens? I cannot advise exact weight or number of blades of grass or lettuce leaves. Mice take only minute portions of vegetables and fruit, and your own experience will be the best judge in determining correct amounts. Your supply should not much exceed the mouse's demand; you want to prevent leftovers from rotting or fermenting in the cage.

Drinking Water

Though mice do not drink very much, some water should be available at all times, since their predominantly dry food does not provide them with the little moisture they do need. No cage should therefore be without a demand-type water dispenser so that the mice may drink a few drops of clean water whenever they wish. Water in a bowl or trough will be contaminated by bedding, droppings, or urine within just a few minutes.

The water bottle does not have to be very big, since you should change the water at least twice a week. In warm weather the water must be changed daily.

Since mice are hypersensitive to chlorine and other chemicals often found in tap water, I recommend either letting the water sit awhile or boiling it before giving it to the animals. Or, better yet, filter your water. If you don't have an automatic filter on your faucets, you can buy easy-to-use filters in drug or health food stores. Non-carbonated mineral water or spring water is also suitable drinking water for mice. Water should have a very low sodium content, otherwise in the long run the mice will take in too much salt.

Diet and Nutrition

The Correct Way to Feed Mice

Mice like routine in their daily activities. Feed your mice at the same time every day. They'll get used to it quickly and will soon even be waiting for you. The actual time depends on your own daily routine; just try to make it a habit to stick to the same feeding time. It's good for the animals—and for you—because that way, you won't forget any feedings.

Fruits and vegetables should always be fresh. Wash them well whether they come from a store or from your own backyard. Any preservatives, pesticides, or contamination by other animals may poison your delicate pets or cause diseases. After washing, shake off excess water from the greens and fruits, or dry them before giving them to the mice, and promptly remove any wilted or shriveled leftovers.

Mouse Care—Some Basics

Coming Home

When you buy a single mouse in a pet shop, the salesperson will probably put the mouse into one of the small cardboard boxes also used for birds. For air supply these boxes are provided with small slits or holes. There are mice who will immediately start gnawing at exactly those locations, and within minutes the hole is large enough to let the mouse squeeze through. Such a situation can prompt a news report about a white mouse running briskly along a crowded street, or scurrying through a bus or subway car. Moral: Place the traveling box with your mouse into a bag or other secure container and keep your eye on it to prevent escape.

If you are buying several mice at once, the shop or the breeder will usually give you a more sturdy wooden traveling case that has a wire mesh top or side. It is not as easy for the mice to escape from one of these.

For a long trip home place some food on the bottom of the case; the animals won't go hungry and can pass the time with pleasant nibbling.

Adjustment Period

When you arrive at home, your mouse will probably still be frightened from the trip. You can help your pet by placing it immediately into its new house (which you have furnished and prepared *in advance,* naturally). Just leave the newcomer alone for awhile. Your mouse will appreciate a little hay or straw on the bottom of the cage—to hide in. From this protective cover, it will observe the new surroundings and collect first impressions; you should not disturb the animal during this time. After about one to three hours, the mouse will come out of hiding and use its teeth to rip away at the hay and straw, either to build a nest or to take a little snack. Now you may approach the cage and put your hand inside to get the mouse used to the way you smell. To avoid scaring the animal it is very important that you do not move at first. The offered hand especially should be kept still for the mouse to sniff at. In time, you can move your hand, always slowly and smoothly; otherwise the mouse will scamper fearfully into a corner.

Do not put your pet's sleeping box into the cage during those first days of adjustment; just provide nesting material. Otherwise, your mouse might hide in the little house and not become tame or will become tame only very slowly.

A tempting delicacy will quickly lure a mouse into your hand for taming.

Mouse Care — Some Basics

How to Tame Your Mouse

In my experience, a mouse needs one or two days to get used to its new surroundings. Right after this initial adjustment, you should start taming the animal. You will know immediately upon putting your hand into the cage whether your mouse is still timid or has become somewhat comfortable with you. If it hides in its nest under the nesting material, or in a corner, it is still afraid. If it remains in the open, waiting, or if, even better, it sniffs at your hand, it trusts you a little, and you have won the first round.

During your taming efforts, take literally the saying, "Good bait catches fine mice." Try placing some delicacy between your fingertips and holding the bait into the cage. If your mouse is still timid, take its food supply away one to two hours before you try the baiting. By that time, the mouse is hungry enough to take the enticing tidbit from your fingers without much hesitation. A little later, place the bait onto your palm, forcing the mouse to place at least its forefeet on your hand. Usually it does not take too long for your mouse to sit right in your palm, eating its reward without showing any fear.

Now is the time to start stroking and petting the mouse very softly with a finger of your other hand. A mouse likes being petted, particularly on its back, neck, and head—that is, on all those places of its body it cannot reach with its tongue, teeth, or feet. Mice are extremely clean animals, constantly grooming themselves, or, within a colony setting, one another (see page 68).

To pick up a mouse, you might try to let it slip into a small cup.

Since a single mouse pet is missing these "grooming partners," it is your job to take their place. Your mouse will soon await this loving service eagerly, letting you stroke it wherever you please.

How to Pick Up Mice

Picking up a mouse that is not yet completely tame is a difficult enterprise at times; you have to get hold of the mouse first. Any awkward handling can be painful enough for a mouse that it will react by biting in shock and fear. For that reason, large-scale breeders and dealers grab mice by the tail or the skin of their necks. Both methods are unpleasant for the animals, but at least not painful. However, using these methods with your pet mouse will make taming much harder; in fact, some animals

Mouse Care — Some Basics

might never become friendly with you. A mouse keeper should therefore grab his pet mice by their tail or the base of their necks only in a dire emergency.

You should not have problems picking up a mouse that has begun to be friendly and will come to eat from your hand. If the mouse is still a little timid, put your hand in front of the animal in the cage, cupping the hand into a slightly opened fist. Usually your mouse will slip into your cupped hand and let itself be picked up. If that does not work yet, try a cup or a small flower pot; a mouse will gladly explore such a "cave."

How to Hold and Carry Mice

Carrying a mouse in your hand correctly is very simple. A mouse will hardly ever jump from a height of more than two feet; it will just sit there quietly. Keep your hand cupped so that your pet cannot fall off accidentally or become frightened of the height. Should you be the one feeling insecure about this, try a little box at first,

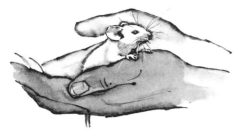

This is the correct way to carry your mouse. In cupped hands, it feels secure and cannot fall.

A shirt pocket—favorite place of many mice—should be loose enough not to pinch the animal.

maybe holding your other hand over it for protection. Remember, mice are extremely curious creatures and will slip into almost anything. It might even happen that your mouse disappears into your sleeve. You might enjoy such behavior, but for many people, this could be a rather disturbing experience. It is therefore a good idea not to hand your mouse to someone about whose reactions you are not absolutely sure. It can be dangerous for the animal because a scared or startled person might fling a mouse away in horror.

Children sometimes like to carry a mouse around in a shirt pocket, or even a trouser pocket. It seems that the mouse likes it just as much. But you do have to watch that the pocket is not too tight, so that the animal won't be pinched or smothered. There have been too many accidents of this kind, so please point out the danger to children. Children really love their animals but sometimes do not realize the consequences of inadvertent carelessness.

Mouse Care — Some Basics

Play and Attention

Mice are extremely active animals. Within a communal mouse family, they often play with each other. They have their favorite games: a little nudge here, a quick lick there, teasing, chasing, and grooming one another.

Since a single pet mouse does not have the opportunity to play with mouse comrades, you, as its caretaker, have to provide this attention. As I recommended earlier, pet and stroke your mouse as much as possible. Take it into your cupped hands frequently. The mouse will also like to use you as a running field. In this play, it won't just climb all over you; it also has many things to explore. Pockets attract it like a magnet. If it regularly discovers a choice morsel in a certain pocket, it will soon find the easiest and shortest way to that pocket. Games of this kind keep a mouse active and challenge its instincts and intelligence. The most important activities, however, are those that substitute for the missing body contact with other mice: stroking a mouse, petting it, and holding it in your warm hands.

A mouse is definitely able to learn: Build your mouse a maze, complete with dead-end corridors and confusing passages leading to a finish line where a reward is waiting. You will be surprised how fast your mouse learns to find its way through the maze in order to get to the reward.

The mouse is an even faster learner when it comes to keeping its balance on steps, ladders, narrow planks, or ropes. It will run up or down, back or forth, de-pending on what you have taught it. But in order to get a mouse to do these things, first you have to get it used to your pocket and to your hands.

The animal will soon regard your shirt pocket as a refuge, its very own place, and your cupped hand as a means of transportation to that refuge. This makes training easier. You can show your mouse the way to its haven via climbing equipment just by placing your hand wherever you want the mouse to go. If you allow it actually to jump into your hand, and from thence into your pocket, the mouse will appreciate this reward.

One particular game never fails to impress spectators—a mouse running up a board with a number of holes. The mouse will slip through one hole after another, in snakelike movements, rather than climb up on one side of the board. A favorite tidbit in your hand will encourage the pet even more to get to the assigned goal—your hand.

Though mice are not as intelligent as their close relatives, the brown rats, they are capable of learning little tricks. For the animals, these games are a welcome change in their daily activities and are part of their fitness training. The trainers—particularly children—enjoy the learning process of their pets tremendously, more so because these lessons are almost always crowned by success. With a little patience on your part, your mice can learn so much that you and your ''mouse circus'' will be highly acclaimed for the entertainment and joy you provide. Children are not only fascinated spectators; but also with the right guidance excellent animal trainers.

Mouse Care — Some Basics

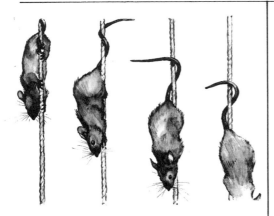

Mice are acrobatic climbers. They even climb up and down a rope, holding on with their tails on the way down.

These performances should always remain fun for the mice and never be associated with force or stress. The routine should last no longer than half an hour twice a day. If you take the natural abilities of mice (running and climbing) into consideration, and if you reward your pets' efforts regularly, the mice will gladly cooperate. This attention from you enriches their lives, making it more interesting than being locked in their cage without rapport with their caretaker—you.

The Run of the House

A small white or colored mouse does not really need a "mouse-run" extending all over the house. It is quite content to climb up and down its owner and do its racing on a table. With a big enough cage, additional running space is also not necessary. On the other hand, the desire to explore the surroundings is characteristic, and it is a good idea to let your pet express its curiosity by running free for a little while each day. Putting your mouse on the rug will not cause it to dart into the nearest nook as a wild house mouse would do. Pet mice have been bred not to display this timidity. Your mouse will move rather slowly, and you can always entice it to slip back into your hand or into a cup. On the other hand, it is not a good idea to let the mouse have the run of your house without supervision. It will become more cautious, more timid, and faster with every free day, soon making it almost impossible to catch it again.

Once one of my mice escaped from its cage. It had access to four rooms (including office and bird room) with furniture and equipment. During the first few days, I moved a lot of furnishings. I saw my scurrying mouse a few times but was never able to catch it. Every time I thought I had finally cornered it, it seemed to disappear from the face of the earth. After a week, I separated the rooms by means of 18-inch high plastic boards and placed food and water in each room to find out which room the mouse was hiding in. During the next "raid," I did find its food warehouse behind the refrigerator, but not a trace of my mouse. Now I divided this room into four parts with the same plastic boards, again with food and water in each one. After finding the area with missing food the next morning, and after partially emptying my sacks of supplies and rearranging my equipment, I finally did find the mouse. At

Mouse Care — Some Basics

first, it raced timidly for any available cover; finally, it just gave up and let me pick it up. It was soon as tame as it had been before the great excursion.

Cleaning of Cage and Accessories

Of all small animals, the house mouse, whether wild or bred, has one of the weakest defense systems against disease, especially infections. To protect your white or colored mouse from disease, it is critically important to be meticulous about cleanliness.

Since the odor of mouse urine is unpleasant, it will soon remind you of your duties. But try to make it a habit to clean cage and accessories before they start smelling. It does not take much time. Cleanliness is the best guarantee for the continued good health of your pet.

Depending on the size of your cage, change the bedding every two days or twice a week (see **page 22**). Weekly washing of cage and accessories with a disinfectant is a proven method of protecting mice from disease. A disinfectant spray without a propellant may be used. Your pet shop has a selection of disinfectants safe for mice and other pets. Let the experts advise you; do not indiscriminately choose a cleaning agent you might use for housecleaning. Disinfectants suitable for animals will also rid your mouse of parasites that are responsible for communicating diseases (see **page 40**). Food containers have to be cleaned daily, drinking water bottles with every change of water (every second day or at least twice a week). Wilted greens and soiled gnawing material should be replaced immediately.

When Your Mouse Becomes Ill

Prevention Is the Best Medicine

Given appropriate housing, care, and nutrition, mice rarely become ill. Though these little rodents are susceptible to a number of diseases, most often, neglect and inappropriate housing are at fault if a mouse contracts an illness.

The best preventive measures are careful observation and consistent, continuous good care for the animals. If you handle your animals every day, watching their behavior and their appearance, you will immediately notice any change. Usually you will even know what is wrong with a particular mouse, and you'll be able to help it before it becomes seriously ill. Attentive observation is therefore the best disease preventive.

In many cases, a simple household remedy may help a sick mouse, or you can clearly detect the reason for your mouse's indisposition and can counteract it. However, if you are not sure why your pet is unwell you should take it to a veterinarian. Only a vet can help with a serious disease, or reassure you that there is nothing seriously wrong with your mouse.

Lack of physical activity and an unbalanced diet are the most frequent causes of illnesses attributable to a mouse owner. Mice are by nature extremely agile and active. If their cage is much too small, or if an exercise wheel and toys are missing, mice will become lazy and obese. In addition, animals kept this way are often also fed the wrong diet; they receive fat cheeses, bacon, cake, or even chocolate and other sweets. No wonder they look like a stuffed sausage after a while, sit around in their cage, and are out of breath with every little activity. Such negligent and thoughtless treatment comes close to cruelty to animals. Slowly but surely, these mice will become ill and will have to endure much unnecessary suffering. Their lifespan, in any case short, will be curtailed.

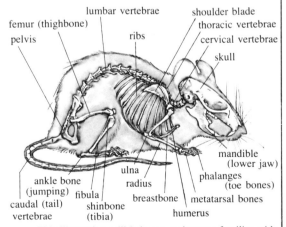

femur (thighbone)
pelvis
lumbar vertebrae
ribs
shoulder blade
thoracic vertebrae
cervical vertebrae
skull
mandible (lower jaw)
phalanges (toe bones)
metatarsal bones
humerus
breastbone
radius
ulna
shinbone (tibia)
fibula
ankle bone (jumping)
caudal (tail) vertebrae

This illustration will help you to become familiar with the parts of a mouse skeleton; such knowledge is an advantage in case of injury and in any discussion with a veterinarian.

Deficiency Diseases

Mice quickly develop symptoms of nutritional deficiencies if their food is old and therefore poor in vitamin content. Seeds of concentrated feed (see **page 25**) must still be capable of germinating to contain vitamins and other active substances needed to prevent deficiency diseases. Greens and fruits are as important as a certain amount of animal proteins.

Deficiencies can be prevented with suitable vitamin supplements that supply the mice with minerals, trace elements, and vitamins by way of the drinking water. By the time a deficiency is severe enough for you to spot it, it is extremely hard to cure. For that reason, it is very important to assure your animals good nutrition with a variety of foods.

Vitamin Deficiency

A deficiency of *vitamin A* primarily causes skin and fur problems or vision disorders, and it may even lead to cramps or paralytic conditions. Carrots, all fresh green vegetables, bananas, and other fruits contain provitamin A; pure vitamin A is found in egg yolk.

A deficiency in vitamins of the *vitamin B complex* can be responsible for various diseases, the most serious being intestinal disorders with diarrhea and emaciation (abnormal loss of weight), disturbance of growth, paralysis, and cramps. Wheat germ, bran, yeast flakes, greens, and fruits are sources of vitamin B.

Mice themselves are capable of producing *vitamin C* and will therefore never lack it. In addition, green food (parsley), fruits, and carrots contain sufficient vitamin C.

Just like children, mice suffering from *vitamin D* deficiency show all the typical symptoms of rickets. In young animals, you can clearly detect soft bones, deformations, and growth retardation. These defi-

ciency symptoms can be attributed to malnutrition (old grain, insufficient oily seeds, and inadequate green fodder). On the other hand, as happens all too often, if a mouse is given too many oily seeds, it gets an overabundance of vitamin D. This decalcifies the bones, which become highly susceptible to fractures, and the calcium forms deposits in the animal's organs and leads to urinary poisoning.

Vitamin E could be called a "fertility vitamin." A deficiency in vitamin E will result in infertility, death of any offspring prior to birth, growth and balance problems, and paralytic conditions. Fresh whole wheat germ contains a high concentration of this vitamin; another good source is egg yolk.

Like all other rodents, mice produce *vitamin K* with the aid of their intestinal bacteria. For that reason, mice do not need any dietary supplement of vitamin K. Green fodder also contains this vitamin. An additional supply is needed only in cases where the normal intestinal flora have been damaged by antibiotics or sulfonamides (administered because of illness). Vitamin K promotes blood coagulation. Symptoms of vitamin K deficiency are intestinal bleeding, nosebleeds, slow healing of injuries, and stunted growth of young animals.

Deficiency of Trace Elements and Minerals

In addition to vitamins, minerals and trace elements are essential for healthy bone structure and metabolism in mice.

When Your Mouse Becomes Ill

Normal bone development requires, above all, a balanced supply of *calcium* and *phosphorus*. Both of these minerals affect metabolism, heart and nerve activity, milk production, and many other essential body functions. An unbalanced diet severely disrupts this mineral balance. Too high a percentage of calcium results in the softening of bones and calcium deposits in internal organs; a deficiency in phosphorus causes nerve and brain damage. You can ensure a healthy balance between calcium and phosphorus by adding a vitamin supplement to the mouse's drinking water or by mixing the supplement into the concentrated feed. All-purpose pellets (see page 26) provide a balanced intake of these minerals.

There is a reciprocal effect between *potassium* and *sodium*, two additional important minerals. Potassium aids in the extraction of body fluids and inhibits the highly stimulating effect of sodium (including the increased retention of body fluids). Sodium, on the other hand, stimulates heart activity and promotes the digestion of proteins. Almost all vegetable foods—that is, grains as well as greens—contain sufficient amounts of potassium.

We call *magnesium, iron, cobalt, iodine,* and many other substances trace elements because only minute amounts of them are needed to guarantee healthy metabolism and normal body functions. However, the absence of one of these trace elements can cause serious deficiency symptoms; the longer the deprivation, the more serious the disease. Fresh grain feed, green vegetables, and vitamin supplements are all sources of these important elements.

Infectious Diseases

Mice can be infected by a number of different disease-causing organisms, including bacteria, viruses, and protozoa. Salmonella and related bacteria are responsible for the most serious infectious mouse diseases. Unclean cage conditions, contaminated feed or water, sour milk or wet greens, and the introduction of diseased animals as well as flies and parasites activate or transmit the disease-causing agents. Diarrhea is one infectious disease that may be caused by a number of different organisms. Antibiotics help combat may in-

Give medication with great care; otherwise the mouse may choke. It is practical to use a syringe or dropper to release the medication drop by drop into the corners of the mouth.

When Your Mouse Becomes Ill

fections but many progress so fast that help will be too late. In addition laboratory examination of the mouse's excrement is needed to identify the disease-causing agent and then determine the medication required to fight it.

If only one of several mice shows symptoms of a disease, isolate the affected animal immediately. In this way, you just might prevent the disease from spreading. Infectious diseases usually do not respond at all to simple remedies, but require veterinary care. However, animal charcoal, black tea, oats, and a multivitamin supplement (from a veterinarian or pet shop) may alleviate symptoms to some degree.

Colds and Infectious Catarrh

As a result of severe changes in temperature, drafts, and high humidity, mice often come down with a cold. There are rather harmless colds that can be cured quickly by protecting the animal's cage from drafts, keeping the temperature steady at approximately 68°F (20°C), and feeding a vitamin preparation.

However, there is also a dangerous and contagious disease that, in the beginning stages, looks like a harmless cold but can destroy whole broods. The pathogenic agents (germs) responsible for this disease belong to the mycobacteria that cause extremely contagious diseases. The animals contaminate one another by sneezing and by touch. This coldlike disease is called "infectious catarrh," or chronic murine pneumonia. It shows all the symptoms of a common cold: squeaking to rattling breath,

In many cases, infrared therapy will help ill mice. The cage temperature should not exceed 86°F (30°C) during treatment.

usually accompanied by a runny nose and watering eyes. The animals sit around, are inactive, have arched backs and bristling fur, and finally start losing hair. The nose becomes increasingly swollen, and breathing more labored. Most of the infected animals will die, because no effective medication has yet been developed against these bacteria. Following exposure to infection, it takes about 10 to 14 days for the disease to break out. After that, it progresses very rapidly, and, unfortunately, gives the animals little chance of survival.

Parasites

Mice are susceptible to many different ectoparasites—that is, organisms living on the outer surface of its host, such as biting fur lice, mites, fleas, and sucking body lice. Some of these only cause itching, or damage the fur somewhat. Others, however, may transmit serious infectious diseases or may severely weaken the animals (especially babies) by their bloodsucking activity.

Many mice have biting lice and mites. An affected mouse should be sprayed immediately with an insecticide available from your vet or pet shop. For about two to three weeks, keep this mouse separate from other mice. Within this time, repeat the treatment twice in order to kill any hatching eggs.

Biting lice (Mallophaga) live in the fur and on the skin and feed on both. They cause severe itching by crawling along the skin. A mouse's scratching then leads to bald patches, skin inflammation, and finally eczema, sometimes even open bleeding wounds. Without treatment, the general condition of the mouse will deteriorate to such a degree that it will die of pneumonia.

Mites often attack in large numbers, and you can't detect them with the naked eye because of their minute size. They cause scales and eczema, particularly in the areas of mouth, nose, and ears. Severe infestations can result in life-threatening infections that are increasingly difficult to cure.

Fleas and sucking body lice attack mice less often. In case of an infestation, the mice scratch and bite themselves and may become extremely susceptible to infections because of loss of blood.

Pest control of fleas, in particular, which hide in every possible nook and crevice, is a very tedious and usually not totally suc-cessful campaign if you use the customary sprays or powders. An insecticide strip seems to be more effective. For three to four months the strips give off a gas that is harmless to mice, other vertebrates, and humans, but fatal to fleas, lice, and many other ectoparasites. Rooms containing such strips should be aired daily, however.

These strips even show good results if you hang them up for just a week or two, remove them, and then reapply them for another week. Airtight packaging keeps them potent and reusable. An added advantage is that they offer the most effective means to keep flies away from mice. That is very important because the common housefly as well as blowflies and their relatives are the main carriers of contagious diseases and parasites to mice.

Worms

Mice can be affected by tapeworms and roundworms (nematodes), but these seldom cause death or even serious illness. However, it is sometimes not recognized that symptoms such as loss of weight, anemia, diarrhea, listlessness, or dull fur are caused by worms. **Should you find any worms or parts of worms in the droppings of your mice, ask your vet for a proper deworming medication.** Worms infesting mice are not transmitted to humans.

Skin Diseases

Most skin diseases are the result of mite infestation. Scratching promotes inflammation, eczema, or open wounds. Skin diseases and mange are difficult to cure even after their cause, the mites, has been removed. An affected mouse should therefore definitely be treated by a veterinarian.

A deficiency in essential amino acids is an additional cause for dermatitis and skin ulcers. These conditions naturally have a detrimental effect on the fur. Amino acids are contained in foods rich in protein, particularly in animal proteins. Mice need only small amounts of protein, but the food containing it must be of high quality and fresh.

Hereditary Diseases

For a layperson, "waltzing" is the most conspicuous congenital disease. It is a behavior caused by brain defects and defects of the pituitary gland and of the middle ear (see "Waltzing Mice," page 13). Dwarfism, another hereditary disease, can occur in conjunction with waltzing or alone. Instead of developing normally, the mice just stop growing at a certain point. Many of these animals die; the survivors' vitality in no way compares to that of normal mice. Deafness is another condition usually occurring in conjunction with waltzing.

There are a few mice families whose litters include a relatively high percentage of mice born with tail malformations: The tail might be bent, or too short, or swollen at one point, or even split into two ends. These conditions are unquestionably hereditary.

Bald mice, often sold as so-called "naked mice," are nothing more than animals affected by a hereditary disease. Absence of fur is a hereditary, sometimes recessive, mutative loss.

Many hereditary diseases are not recognized as such but are attributed to incorrect care, housing, or nutrition. Epilepsy, paralysis, cramps, and noisy breathing may be inherited conditions. Clubfeet, missing or extra toes, and a number of other congenital deformities are also often inherited.

Many anomalies are detectable *before* you buy an animal: you can see which mice you should not buy because of obvious hereditary defects—missing toes, for example. This proves again that inspection is extremely important in choosing your pet mice.

Tooth deformities are frequently hereditary. In one such disorder, the upper and lower incisors do not grow towards each other, with the result that their cutting surfaces do not have the sharpening and abrasive action normally achieved by gnawing. The upper incisors curve backwards, growing back into the mouth in an ever-increasing arc, while the lower incisors often grow straight up, out of the mouth. Pinching off these malformed teeth is only a temporary solution; usually, the condition worsens with time. The teeth continue to grow apart until it becomes impossible for the animal to eat anything. Molars may also be affected by irregular growth, but the consequences of that condition are not quite so serious.

I could go on and tell you about other hereditary diseases, but I don't want to scare you. I did think it important to introduce you to the subject so that you will not inadvertently contribute to the propagation of diseased animals. Inbreeding is the main cause for these defects. Stay away from inbreeding, because a hobby breeder cannot be certain about any hereditary defects an animal might harbor. If you are breeding colored mice, and pairing unrelated animals, there is little danger of hereditary disease. Colored mice destined as pets for mice fanciers are usually healthy animals full of vitality; it is rare for such a mouse to be affected by any hereditary disease.

Internal Injuries

An accidental fall or an inadvertent kick or hard squeeze may result in internal injuries. If your mouse has difficulty moving or sitting, you should take it to a vet immediately. During the trip, put the mouse carefully onto a soft material, like a towel, preferably on the animal's side, in a small basket or other suitable hard container.

If you believe that your mouse has not sustained internal injuries, put it into its cage and observe it. It might be suffering temporary shock. Should you notice any change in your pet's behavior, however, particularly in the way it moves, ask your vet for advice. The presence of any internal injuries might otherwise cause the animal prolonged pain.

Other Disorders

Mice are subject to certain other disorders, some of which may be the result of a metabolic defect. Among other disorders of mice are broken and overgrown teeth.

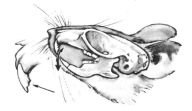

You can distinguish a house mouse from its closest relatives, the wood mouse and the yellow-necked mouse, by the characteristic projection on the back of the upper incisors.

Broken Teeth
Mineral deficiencies (of calcium particularly) may cause an incisor to just break off. Vitamin supplements or a calcium preparation are the answer. Should your mouse have a recurring problem of breaking teeth, however, consult your vet, who may be able to help with an injection, since the animal's system is obviously incapable of sufficiently metabolizing the minerals given by way of food.

Overgrown Teeth
Given the right nourishment, it is rare that the incisors of a healthy mouse grow too long. Gnawing on hard kernels and dry bread keep the teeth to a normal length. In addition, upper and lower teeth are wearing each other down (see illustration). Should your mouse's incisors become too long despite correct feed and abrasive action, a veterinarian is able to clip them.

Mother mice and their young.
Top: Red-backed mouse and wild house mouse.
Bottom: White mouse (albino mouse).

When Your Mouse Becomes Ill

Symptoms of Old Age

Mice may exhibit signs of old age when they are between one and three years old, depending on the vitality of the individual mouse and on that of its breeding strain. These symptoms can vary considerably. They usually begin with a decrease in a mouse's physical activity, a less glossy coat, and decreased appetite, followed by an arched back, bald spots, and eczema. The probability of tumors, benign as well as malignant, increases in time, and some animals progressively lose weight before their eventual death.

Recent strains of colored mice:
Top: Cream-colored long-haired mouse and recessive black-and-white marked long-haired mouse.
Center: Natural-colored recessive marked and recessive black-and-white marked.
Bottom: Silver-colored mouse and tan brown mouse (brown with tan underside).

Breeding and Reproduction

Mice keepers who would like *just once* to observe the estrus (period of heat), mating, and gestation of their pet house mouse, and the birth, development, and rearing of its young—who, in short, want to get an impression of the family life of mice—should have no problem finding good homes for the offspring among relatives and friends. If you want more than this one-time breeding experiment, however, always remember the following warning: The house mouse multiplies so fast that, in no time at all, you won't know where to put the hordes of mice! Random, unsystematic breeding should therefore be avoided. If you have colored mice, be particularly careful and discreet about mating your mice, and inquire at several pet shops whether they would be willing to take any surplus offspring. The following recommendations for breeding and propagation are designed to help the conscientious mouse keeper to enjoy breeding his or her pets.

Breeding Requirements

Anyone wishing to breed mice has to realize that, even though these tiny creatures might not need much room, you cannot raise them in a storage closet, much less your kitchen! In addition, the typical mouse odor is already apparent with just one pair of mice and their litter. People do not appreciate this odor, so do not breed even one pair in the living room, bedroom, or the nursery. An unoccupied room is best, and since mice are not too particular in this respect, the attic or basement are a good choice. The only requirements are that the chosen room is neither too hot nor too cold, neither too dry nor too humid, nor too dark.

Many people point out that wild house mice spend all day in their dark hiding places, becoming active mainly at night. Why then do pet mice need light, they ask. The fact is that experiments have shown mice to be most comfortable with 12 hours daily of either shaded natural light (no direct sun) or artificial light.

Good ventilation is a further requirement; fresh air is extremely important for the well-being of the animals. Fresh air does not mean drafty air; drafts can make mice ill as easily as considerable changes in temperature. Mice thrive in a constant normal room temperature of 68° to 72°F (20°–22°C) and a humidity of 50% to 60%. These requirements should be met for any breeding program, whether you are trying to breed whole colonies of mice or just one or two pair.

Systems of Breeding

There are two basic breeding programs—the monogamous system and the harem system. With either system the requirements for breeding and guidelines for selecting breeding stock are the same.

Monogamous Pair System

A large mouse cage like the one described on **page 20** is sufficient for breed-

Breeding and Reproduction

ing a single pair of mice. The basic requirements regarding accessories and care are the same whether you have a pair of mice, a single one, or two mice of the same sex. For breeding, the animals need nesting material like grass, hay, straw, or unprinted paper. To feel secure, breeding stock should definitely have a little nesting house made of wood or cardboard, or even plastic. If you prefer plastic, provide a house without a floor, though. Because of the body heat of the animals, humidity may condense on the walls of a plastic house; this invites the growth of bacteria and mold. Unpainted wood and cardboard, on the other hand, can dissipate any moisture.

When we are dealing with just one pair of mice, they will normally be tame and accustomed to people. The mice will not become timid on cleaning day (once or twice a week, depending on the size of the cage and the nature of the bedding). If you'd like to be able to clean the cage without having to bother the animals for any length of time, you might consider having two similar cages, exchanging cages whenever it's cleaning time. This way, you can clean the soiled cage thoroughly at your leisure.

You will need at least two more cages if your breeding of one pair is not to result in an endless mouse population explosion. At an age of 21 to 25 days, the young have to be separated by sex; if you wait for more than four weeks, your females may be pregnant already.

Monogamous breeding with several different pairs of mice is the procedure to use

if you want to breed selected color shades. But you do have to know the genetic characteristics of each animal in order to be able to obtain the desired mutations. In addition, this kind of breeding requires keeping exact records for each animal.

One more tip: Have the baby mice reared by an individual pair already accustomed to people. After all, they will become pets of your friends or of other people by way of a pet shop, and their owners will be delighted to receive tame mice. You tame the babies by handling them frequently once they are 12 days old. During the so-called "leap age" or "flea age," at about 16 days, it is particularly easy to get mice used to humans. When they grow up, they will be much tamer than mice from a litter with no human contact or little human contact. During the "leap age" mice take remarkably high jumps and leaps—hence the name; take care, therefore, that the mice don't give you the slip or hurt themselves.

Harem System

Breeding strains or colonies of mice is advisable only for breeders who need large numbers of mice for purposes such as supplying professional pet dealers. This breeding method involves housing one male mouse and two to five females in a single large cage. The females, called *does,* give birth to their litters in a communal setting, often even in common nests. They usually get along very well if they live together from an early age. Once such a harem group is established, it should be kept intact. Adding other females at a later time may result in fighting.

If the females have the same coloration and genetic heritage, you won't be able to determine which young are from which mother. If your goal is to breed certain color strains, you have two choices: You can either stock one harem with females of different colors, making it possible to differentiate between the babies, or you can place each pregnant doe in a separate smaller cage a few days before her due date. After about 21 days (see "Nest Building and the Raising of Litters," page 70), the female is returned to the breeding community. This procedure ensures that your females will give birth only every 45 to 60 days. If you leave them with the males constantly, including the nursing period, they can have a litter every 20 to 30 days, since mice will be in heat even when they are nursing.

You can use the harem system with larger groups of animals as well, but a maximum number of five females seems to be the most practical for hobby breeders. An additional possibility is that of combining two to three males and four to twelve females in one colony. In such a breeding system, however, the males often fight for dominance, and often a single male, the "lead buck," mates with all the females (see "Fighting for Rank and Territory," page 69). Besides, such large groups of mice will produce so many young that a hobby breeder would be hard pressed to house and sell them. For purposes of odor control, mice breeding of this magnitude requires quite a bit of space in quarters far removed from your home and from your neighbors. No matter how thorough your cleaning efforts and how good the ventilation system, the typical mouse odor will prevail.

Selecting Mice for Breeding

The vitality and growth rate of stud mice is an important breeding factor. Your mice should come from healthy, resistant stock. For that reason, it is advisable to get your animals from a good breeder or a pet shop owner who is also a mouse breeder. These sources offer a better selection, and it is easier to obtain mice with compatible characteristics or even mice who are used to one another already.

You will, naturally, check the animal's health very carefully. Do not buy any animals with dull, unkempt fur or arched backs. Blurry or inflamed eyes are a sign of possible disease; so are diarrhea or a soiled backside. Neither obese nor emaciated mice are suitable for breeding, nor are those who keep their head at an angle, are lame, or have waltzing tendencies.

Heat and Mating

An unpregnant female is in heat every three to six days. At that time, her vagina remains open for a period of approximately twelve hours; at other times, it is closed by a mucous plug. The estrous cycle depends on the age of the animal; young females have shorter cycles; older ones, longer cycles.

Breeding and Reproduction

A mouse buck sniffs and licks a doe in heat and follows her around, trying to cover her. If the female is in a mating mood, she raises her backside and turns the tail a little to the side. Mating takes only a few seconds, but it is repeated several times.

Keeping a mouse pair—or a mouse harem—constantly together results in a repetitive reproductive rhythm. A female who gives birth to a litter will normally be in heat again within 24 hours. Thus the females are almost always pregnant, even when they are nursing a new litter. You can expect another litter in as short a time as three weeks. This normal biological process raises no special concerns. Given the right climate, food supply, and nesting conditions, even a wild house mouse is constantly reproducing. Wild rodents, hunted by both humans and other animals, need numerous offspring for the community to survive. A wild living doe, however, will usually not live long enough to raise 10 to 15 litters with anywhere between 40 and 120 young. If she succeeds in rearing 20 to 30 offspring, she has done her share in ensuring the survival of her species. Pet mice are a different story. Protected from disease and from natural enemies, a doe is able to rear 100 and more young in just 12 to 15 months. One might think that such productivity would overtax the female, but experiments have shown that extended pauses between pregnancies can actually result in complications.

In a communal situation with several males and a larger number of females, the males usually fight for the dominant rank in the social order (see "Social Behavior," page 68). The strongest male gains the prerogative of mating with all females. Subordinate males are tolerated in the colony, but they may not mate. It appears that this subordination causes them to temporarily lose their sex drive. We know that the condition is a temporary one because the males continue to contest the position of the dominant male by fighting. If the mice know each other and if the losers accept the dominance of the strongest male, these fights are rather harmless. If two males of comparatively equal strength are fighting, however, and there is a female in heat, those confrontations can easily end with injuries, or even with the death of one of the rivals.

Mice like to live with their families or in colonies with all of their kin, and they multiply very fast in such a communal family structure. A breeder often has a hard time to stay ahead of the situation and keep in control. For that reason, I would advise any hobby breeder to mate only individual pairs. That way, you always have the choice of either separating a female for the birth and rearing of a litter whenever her pregnancy becomes obvious, or of letting her mate again immediately following the birth of one set of her many children.

Gestation

The gestation, or pregnancy, period of house mice and their domesticated colored relatives usually lasts 18 to 24 days.

Initial development of embryos in the

Breeding and Reproduction

womb is rather slow; you usually cannot tell that a mouse is pregnant until about 15 days into the pregnancy. Some females become extremely large after that; others hardly change. In the latter case, the litter will almost always consist of only a few small young ones.

However, you can tell a doe's pregnancy very soon by the change in her behavior. She becomes restless, collects all sorts of nesting materials, and starts building a nest. Straw, hay, dry leaves, fresh grass, wood chips, unprinted paper strips, and cardboard make good nesting materials, as does the mixture you can buy in pet shops. With her teeth the female shreds everything she deems too coarse, gnawing straw, paper, and cardboard into very fine, soft strips. She builds her nest in the darkest and warmest place she can find. That might be the corner of the cage where you place food and drink, or it might be the sleep house. In many cases, females build a second nest right next to the first one. The purpose might be to act as a decoy for any would-be enemies, but the mice also use this nest for resting and storage.

Take care that you provide a pregnant doe with a dark area, preferably a little nesting house, and sufficient nesting material in plenty of time. The more time a mouse can spend on building a nest for her litter, the busier it can be before giving birth, the better mother it will become.

Birth

With the approximately three-week gestation period almost over, a doe continues with renewed vigor to build the nest where she will give birth. She can throw her litter at any time, day or night, but most births take place between 10 PM and 2 AM. The birth itself usually lasts about half an hour, even though a small litter (1 to 5) might take as little as 15 minutes, while a very large one (15 to 22) may take longer. While giving birth, the mother is squatting, receiving each of her babies in turn. She grabs the skin "packaging" of each new arrival, rips it open, and bites off the umbilical cord. She immediately starts licking the newborn until it is clean, eats the sac and afterbirth, and then starts taking care of the next arrival in the same manner.

At the end of the birthing process, all her young are lying underneath her, clean and meticulously arranged, their pink skin dry and warm (see color photo on page 45). The mouse continues to lick her litter for quite a while, particularly along the underside of the new arrivals, not forgetting their mouths, their noses, or their tiny rear ends.

During the first 8 to 10 days, the mother licks away both the urine of her young and the so-called milk excrement—the droppings of newborn mice. Licking is very important; its massaging action stimulates the newborns' digestive functions.

A mother mouse giving birth should never be disturbed. She panics whenever she fears her litter might be in danger, running about the cage in total confusion, carrying the young here, and then there, and dropping them in the process. In her anxiety, she will even eat her young when she cannot find a safe and quiet hiding place for them. For that reason, watching a

Breeding and Reproduction

A newborn mouse is rosy, naked, and blind—and small enough to fit easily into a ring.

mouse giving birth to a litter is risky. Above all, the nest and the newborn should not be touched; even the tamest of mice may become extremely sensitive as a mother. All in all, it is a good idea to keep your understandable curiosity in check and wait a week before taking a peek into the nest. Naturally, there are exceptions. Some mice do not mind at all if you take a look or even handle the new babies. Mice behaving in this manner are, for the most part, older animals who have accepted humans and their odor as a normal fact of mouse environment.

The Development of the Young

Depending on the size of the litter, a newborn mouse weighs between $\frac{1}{28}$ and $\frac{1}{14}$ ounce (1–2 grams). The babies are totally naked and blind. After 2 to 3 days, hair tips start breaking the skin, and after 3 days the ears open. During the first 5 days, the young move only in circles; that way, they won't fall out of a nest, and remain in the vicinity of the nest should one of them be dragged out because the mother is leav-

ing the nest while a baby is still nursing. They react only to heat and to touch, and they will always remain underneath the mother or with their brothers and sisters.

After about a week, a few daring baby mice may venture out of the nest, but the mother carries them back immediately. The fur develops quickly now; mice have all their hair by the time they are 8 to 10 days old. They weigh $\frac{1}{5}$ to $\frac{1}{4}$ ounce (5–7 grams) now. Incisors become visible on day 11 to day 13, and the eyes open between the 12th and 14th day. At this time, the young ones start exploring the nest and its immediate surroundings and begin taking solid nourishment instead of living exclusively on their mother's milk. While their excrement was liquid or semiliquid before, to be licked off by the mother, the babies now have a normal digestion with regular mouse droppings.

At about 16 days, the mice reach the so-called "leap" or "flea age": When you open the cage lid, or when the animals are disturbed in any other way, they may jump straight up into the air to escape any danger.

Should mother mouse have to carry a young one any distance, she grabs it by the abdominal skin. The baby curls up and is easy to transport.

At 15 days, the young mice weigh ¼ to ⅓ ounce (about 7–9 grams); at 20 days, they reach a weight of ⅖ to ³⁄₇ ounce (10–12 grams). They are well developed by now, looking much like their parents, just a little smaller. They continue to gain weight, reaching ³⁄₇ to ⁵⁄₇ ounce (15–20 grams) at the age of 30 days. After approximately 5 to 6 months, the mice are fully grown, a wild house mouse weighing approximately 1 ounce (28 grams). White and colored mice become somewhat bigger; there are animals weighing as much as 2.14 ounces (60 grams). These considerable differences depend on the species, the strain, and on nutrition and care.

At the age of 21 to 25 days, a litter should be separated by sex. Mice are sexually very precocious; the vagina of females opens at the age of 28 to 49 days (see "Heat and Mating," page 50), and young males are ready to mate about 6 to 8 days later.

Breeding Colored Mice

Genetics is the science of heredity. For centuries, humans tried in vain to solve the mysterious puzzle of heredity. It was Gregor Johann Mendel (1822–1884), an Augustinian monk and son of a farmer, who finally succeeded in discovering the basic principles involved in genetics (mainly by crossbreeding garden peas). However, people neither understood nor took note of the treatise Mendel published in 1866 containing a detailed description of his many experiments over a period of many years. It was not until the end of the 19th century that biologists doing the same kind of research, and getting the same results, realized the importance of Mendel's findings. Scientists soon realized that these laws were valid not only for plants but also for animals, including humans. In honor of their discoverer, these principles of heredity were called "Mendel's Laws"; they are still the basis of genetics.

Hereditary transmission can be determined only over several generations. For that reason, mice are perfect for genetic studies because new generations are born faster than in almost any other mammal. Hereditary processes needing years to observe in other animals are evident in only a few months with mice.

Many breeders of mice enjoy breeding colored mice, trying for ever new colors and color combinations. Because of Mendel's Laws, we are now able to breed selectively in any desired color variation. The heredity of colors is an extremely complicated matter, however; Mendel's Laws cannot be explained in a simple manner taking a colored mouse as an example. Unless a hobby breeder knows the genotype of the mice to be bred, that is, the hereditary information coded in the animals' genes (hereditary factors), there is always a chance of surprising results in breeding efforts. Should breeding be based only on the phenotype of the animals, which means their outer appearance and characteristics,

Relatives of the wild house·mouse: yellow-necked mice (top and bottom left); harvest or dwarf mouse (bottom right).

the mating of two apparently black mice just might result in white, black, and chocolate-colored young instead of a probably expected all black litter. You can be reasonably sure only when you are pairing two albino mice; their young will always be white. If you are thinking of breeding new or specific color combinations, an intensive study of genetics is a prerequisite in order to determine your animals' genotype. However, don't lose heart, or the joy of mouse breeding, if you don't succeed in obtaining the desired color effect on the first try.

In a book like this, I can only give you a limited summary of hereditary processes, just enough to whet a hobby breeder's appetite for a more detailed study of genetics.

How Are Colors Transmitted?

Colors, as well as all other hereditary characteristics of all living things, are transmitted in the form of genes (hereditary units). With the union of sperm and ovum, each offspring receives characteristics from each of its parents. In case of two purebred mice of the same color (e.g., albinos), the young will be just like their parents and will also be purebred.

Since individual mice are subject to occasional mutations (sudden gene changes), other colors emerge. In nature, these muta-

Top: harvest mouse in a ball nest (left), yellow-necked mouse nesting in a hollow tree (right). Center: spiny mouse (left) and yellow-necked mouse (right). Bottom: Field mouse (left) and voles in a fight for dominance (right).

tions will usually disappear again, the characteristics of the wild animals being dominant. However, if a breeder emphasizes these color changes on purpose, they may persist as inheritable characteristics. You can determine hereditary processes and utilize them for breeding purposes on the basis of Mendel's Laws.

The *First Mendelian Law* states: If you cross purebred individuals of the same species who differ in only *one* characteristic, all of their offspring (the first filial generation, designated F_1) will be uniform.

The *Second Mendelian Law* states: If you pair the offspring of the first filial generation *with each other*, their offspring (designated F_2) will no longer be uniform but will segregate according to a certain ratio. For instance, in dominant characteristics, the ratio is 3:1. This ratio can be proven only when you breed *many* animals. It is impossible to give you a *simple* example of both of these laws in terms of a mouse color; that would go beyond the purpose of this book.

Long-haired mice (see color photo on page 46), available in England since 1966, in America more recently, are very good subjects for simple and graphic demonstration of hereditary principles according to Mendel's Laws. The reason is that the hereditary factor responsible for long hair is a single gene instead of the many genes involved in the transmission of colors.

If you pair a long-haired mouse and one with short hair, *all* F_1 young will have short hair. According to Mendel's first law, they are uniform. The animals have short hair because, in this case, the short hair is

Breeding and Reproduction

a dominant (stronger) hereditary factor. However, the characteristic for having long hair is by no means lost; it is recessive (hidden) and will emerge again in the next generation. Now, if you pair the F_1 offspring with each other, their offspring will not be uniform; instead, in accordance with Mendel's 2nd law, there will be a segregation according to the ratio for dominant hereditary factors, i.e., a ratio of 3:1 (three animals with dominant short hair, one with recessive long hair).

Color heredity in mice is essentially determined by five different pairs of genes. That is the reason, in the breeding of colored mice, it is so hard to predict which color genes will act together when you cross certain colors with each other. In this area, the British hobby breeders have organized into chapters of a national organization (National Mouse Club–see page 75) and have quite some literature at their disposal helping them to understand genetics in order to be able to breed certain desired colors.

There is a genetic color classification system based on the laws determining which colors belong together and how they relate to each other (dominant, recessive). Only one color from each class can be present in the genes of any one mouse. The most important class is the one containing the natural colored (gray) mouse. As a parent form, it has the strongest color characteristics. For easier differentiation, the five color classes have been labeled with letters, a capital letter designating a dominant factor, a lower case letter a recessive one. The first color of each class is

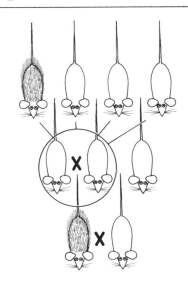

When pairing a short-haired mouse and a long-haired mouse, you cannot expect any long-haired animals until the second generation.

the predominant one, the last one is the least significant color (the most recessive). Since modern mouse breeding started with the British (and with it the experience in the genetics of mice), the letters originally chosen by them have been accepted internationally.

Class A is named after the English agouti, what we usually term natural color or mouse gray. This class includes:

A^y = dominant yellow (y = yellow)
A^w = natural, white belly (w = white)
A = natural, gray·
a^t = black with tan belly (t = tan)
a = black

Breeding and Reproduction

Brown mice make up the second class B (brown):

B = black
b = brown

The third class, labeled C (for color), covers albino mice:

C = color present (colored mouse)
c^{ch} = chinchilla
c^h = Siamese or Himalayan
c = color missing (albino)

The fourth class is provided for the color dilution factor and designated D (for dilution):

D = full-strength color
d = diluted color

The fifth class contains mice with red eyes (not based on the same mutation as the red eyes of albinos). This is class P (for pink-eyed):

P = normal eyes and color
p = red eyes; brown and black fur colors are diluted

The two piebald or marked factors have no bearing on the color of the mouse, but they have an effect on its distribution; for that reason, they are also called distribution factors. You cannot predict the location of color on the fur of an animal. However, selective breeding can produce mice with similar color distribution. Dominant marked have been designated by Rw (for rump white), recessive ones by s or du (for self, Dutch). An additional hereditary characteristic pertaining to fur instead of color is long hair (designated Gen go for long hair); it surfaced in England in 1966 and was standardized in 1969. Today, long-haired mice can be found almost everywhere, and are recognized in any standardized color.

Main Color Varieties

Dominant yellow (A^yA): This color is dominant over the natural mouse color; the mouse has black eyes and a uniform reddish-yellow color.

White-bellied natural (A^wA^w): This color shade is also a more dominant factor than the natural color. This strain has a white belly.

Natural color (AA): In most pairings, you may expect natural-colored mice, since this shade is dominant over most other colors. The hair roots of these mice are black, followed by a yellow ring; the tips have a yellowish tinge. Most of the whiskers are dark, underlining the agouti effect of the fur.

Tan-bellied black (a^ta^t): The reddish-yellow (tan) hair was preserved on the underparts but not on the back, resulting in this interesting two-toned variety.

Black (aa): This color shade characterizes a mouse that is totally black (even on the underparts).

Black (BB): In this variety, black is dominant. It is the dominant factor in the color class characterizing brown mice.

Brown (aabb): This color is often termed "chocolate."

Cinnamon (AAbb): The shade results from breeding a gray and a brown mouse. However, the color does not emerge until the F_2 generation, F_1 producing only gray mice, since gray dominates brown.

Albino (cc): There are quite a number of strains of white mice with very different hereditary characteristics. A white mouse may have genes for many colors which can be determined by test breeding.

Blue (aaBBdd): This code refers to a black mouse with diluted color (in addition to color, heredity is also affected by the color dilution factor -d-).

Recessive marked (ss or dudu): This mouse with a white blaze on its face, one on its belly, often a third one on its back, exists in all colors. It is a very common pet, and better known as Dutch pied or Dutch marked.

Dominant marked (RwRw): The color distribution of these mice can vary considerably, i.e., a mouse might show a lot of color or very little. Usually, the animal's backside is white, hence the designation ''rump white,'' but it has to have genes for at least one other color. Purebred dominant marked are not viable; they will die after a few days.

The House Mouse and Its Relatives

White mice, colored mice, and waltzing mice are all descendants of the house mouse (*Mus musculus*). Its position within the systematic classification (called taxonomy) is as follows:

Order: Rodents (Rodentia)
Suborder: Mouselike rodents (Myomorpha)
Family: Mice (long-tailed or modern mice; Muridae)
Subfamily: Real, True, or Old World Mice (Murinae)
Genus: Mice (*Mus*)
Species: Common house mouse (*Mus musculus*)

Many varieties of house mice are found in North America, in Europe, in North Africa, and in Asia.

House Mouse Varieties

Common Western (Old World) **House Mouse**   Color photos, pages 10 and 45

Mus musculus domesticus

The Common Western or Old World House Mouse of western Europe is the original, true house mouse, for it is found almost exclusively in buildings. It is closely associated with humans even dependent on humans (see "The House Mouse in Its Natural Habitat," **page 66**). It is found throughout western Europe.

Northern House Mouse

Mus musculus musculus

This mouse can also be found in structures but also inhabits fields and meadows. For that reason, it is often called corn mouse or meadow house mouse. It is found throughout North America; also in southwestern Canada north to central British Columbia, and along the Pacific coast north to Alaska.

Steppe House Mouse

Mus musculus spicilegus

This subspecies lives in the southwest of the Soviet Union and all over the Balkan states. As an inhabitant of the steppes (European prairies), it seldom invades human dwellings but lives mainly on grass seeds and grains. The gray of its back has a more pronounced yellowish hue than that of the Western house mouse; its belly is white.

Asiatic House Mouse

Mus musculus bactrianus

Manchurian House Mouse

Mus musculus manchu

Both of these subspecies inhabit the interior of Asia. Predominantly desert mice, they occasionally become undesired inhabitants of local huts and houses. Their appearance is similar to that of the steppe mice.

Wagnerian House Mouse

Mus musculus wagneri

The Wagnerian house mouse of eastern Asia is as very "homey" species, and just as persis-

The House Mouse and Its Relatives

tent as the common house mouse. Both mice are similar in size and color, and characterized by the same long tail. This mouse might be the ancestor of the Japanese waltzing mouse; it is possible that Portuguese sailors and merchants imported the house mouse to Japan, either by accident or design, more than 300 years ago.

Iberian House Mouse

Mus musculus spretus

The human contact of the Iberian house mouse of Spain, Portugal, and northwestern Africa is not quite as close as that of our common house mouse. Its tail is a little shorter, its color a little more brownish.

Relatives of the House Mouse

In Europe, there are only a few species belonging to the same family as the house mouse.

Striped Field Mouse

Apodemus agrarius

This mouse species lives in swampy thickets, woodlands, and gardens. It has become rare in Western Europe, the western part of its distribution area, but is still common from east of the Elbe all the way across the Ural Mountains. Its reddish-brown coat is characterized by a "brand" marking, a dark streak along its back. With a body length of about 4 to 5 inches (10–13 centimeters), it is larger than the common house mouse. It lives on seeds, roots, and green plants, but also eats small animals such as sow bugs or insects, even earthworms. Most winters, it burrows underground, building a nest and storage chamber, but it will also take refuge in buildings (stables, sheds, or barns). It lives on stored food and does not hibernate during the cold months of the year.

Harvest or Dwarf Mouse

Color photo, pages 55, 56, back cover

Micromys minutus

With a body length of only 2⅜ to 3 inches (6–8 centimeters), a tail of 2 to 2¾ inches (5–7 centimeters), and a weight of about 1/16 to 1/3 ounce (5–10 grams), the harvest mouse is one of the smallest long-tailed mice. Its color is yellow-brown, and it has a prehensile tail for climbing and balancing. High grasses, and oat and wheat fields are its main habitat, where it builds perfectly round, artistically intertwined ball nests between grain stalks or in thickets. It eats primarily grass seeds, roots, and insects. Caught very young, harvest mice make very good pets.

Yellow-Necked Mouse

Color photos, pages 55, 56 back cover

Sylvaemus flavicollis or *Apodemus flavicollis*

With a body length of 3½ to over 5 inches (9–13 centimeters), this mouse is rather big. The tail is as long as the body; the almost bald ears are conspicuously large. The white belly is a sharp contrast to the otherwise brown body of the mouse, a characteristic distinguishing it clearly from the wood mouse. The name derives from a yellow band around its throat. The yellow-necked mouse lives in woods, deciduous forests, and cultivated parks, usually building its nest underground under rocks or tree roots. But nests and stored supplies can also be found

The House Mouse and Its Relatives

in hollow tree trunks and nesting boxes up to 25 feet (7.5 meters) high. It lives on seeds, fruits, berries, and insects. When fleeing, this mouse can jump a distance of more than 3 feet (1 meter). If an enemy should grab its tail, the skin of the tail is cast off, allowing the mouse to escape.

Wood Mouse

Sylvaemus sylvaticus

Despite its name, this mouse species is mostly found on the fringes of fields, on heath and moorlands, dunes, and in pine forests. The gray of its underparts, embellished by a yellow spot, gradually turns into a brown-colored back. The wood mouse lives mainly on grass seeds.

Spiny Mouse

Color photo, page 56

Acomys cahirinus

In Europe, the spiny mouse can be found only on Crete and Cyprus; it is more at home in Egypt and Asia Minor. Like the house mouse, it followed civilization, living on stored grain and other human foodstuffs. Its name alludes to prickly, flattened spines along the middle of its back, which provide better protection against enemies than the soft fur of other mice. The back of these mice is tan, their belly white; their ears are conspicuously long. Spiny mice are another species whose tail breaks off easily, letting them escape from an enemy that grabs their wriggling tail. The young of these mice, usually three to five to a litter, are much better developed than those of other mice. It is said that gestation takes somewhat longer, too, about 26 to 30 days.

House Mouse

Wood Mouse

Meadow or Field Mouse

Harvest Mouse

Black rat

Relative sizes of the house mouse and its closest relatives.

63

The House Mouse and Its Relatives

Black or House Rat

Rattus rattus

The black rat has a body length of approximately 6¼ to 9½ inches (16-24 centimeters) plus a tail of about 7 to almost 10 inches (18–25 centimeters), with 200 to 260 scales. Eyes and ears are larger than those of the brown rat. This rat needs human habitation for survival and lives mainly in attics, stables, and barns. It is a very social creature, living peacefully in family colonies. If it is tamed young, it can become a devoted, trainable, playful pet. This rat is found throughout North America; also in **south Canada to central British Columbia, and** along the Pacific coast north to Alaska.

Brown or Norwegian Rat

Rattus norvegicus

This rat species grows to a length 8¼ to 11 inches (21–28 centimeters), plus a tail of 6¾ to **9 inches (17-23 centimeters) and weighs be-**tween 10 and 19 ounces (about 280–530 grams). The tail always has 160 to 190 scales. Ears and eyes are relatively small. This large rat prefers basements and lower floors; it sometimes makes its home near water. In contrast to the black rat, it likes to swim, but it is not as good a climber as its black relative. It builds underground passages, nests, and stores. While it shows more timidity towards humans, it exhibits extremely aggressive behavior towards house mice and house rats. In its family social order, on the other hand, it is peaceful and caring. (The white rat, crested rat, and all other mutations derive from this brown rat.)

The brown rat is found throughout North America and also in southwest Canada north to central British Columbia, and along the Pacific coast north to Alaska.

Other Mouse Family Relatives

I would like to list just a few of the more distant relatives of the common house mouse here. The reason is that these animals—like voles, for instance— are often confused with the actual house mouse and because some of them—like the American white-footed mouse—make very good pets.

Voles   color photos, **page 56**

Voles (Microtidae) are actually very distant relatives of the common house mouse. Voles form a large family, containing a large variety of rodents of all sizes, including such diverse ones as lemmings, moles, muskrats, and the well known pine mice and field mice. Their habitats are also quite varied. Moles live in fields, gardens, forest, and water; muskrats are water or marsh animals; lemmings, red-backed mice (see photo on **page 45**), snow mice, and mountain mice can live way up in the mountains, even beyond the timber line.

In general, members of the vole family are not very suitable pets. Field mice and pine mice might make cute pets if they become accustomed to humans at an early age, but they never completely lose their timidity. They are animals for a roomy terrarium, to be watched from a distance.

Rock voles, as well as long-tailed and California voles are often taken for house mice. After all, for most people, a mouse is a mouse. To help you differentiate between the two families, here are some of the main differences: As opposed to the house mouse, voles are characterized by a less pointed nose and rather small ears almost totally hidden in the surrounding fur. In addition, the length of a vole's tail is only about half that of a house mouse, usually not even half as long as the body length of the animals.

The House Mouse and Its Relatives

Some North American voles are: Meadow Vole *(Microtus pennsylvanicus)*; Montana Vole (*M. montanus*); California Vole (*M. californicus*); Tundra Vole (*M. oeconomus*); Mexican Vole (*M. mexicanus*); Long-tailed Vole (*M. longicaudus*); Creeping or Oregon Vole (*M. oregoni*) and Woodland Vole (*M. pinetorum*).

North American White-Footed Mouse

The North American white-footed mice, also called deer mice because their colors resemble those of the white-tailed deer, are very similar to the long-tailed mice of Western Europe, but are actually more closely related to the hamsters. They are the commonest small rodents throughout North America. Very common is the deer mouse (*Peromyscus maniculatus*). The animal is found on prairies, in brushy areas, and woodlands. White-footed mice belong to the genus *Peromyscus* (with about 15 different species). Their underside and feet are white; they have big ears and a very long tail.

White-footed mice are bred in different colors in the United States: gray, yellow, and white (albinos). Their disadvantages are that they need a lot of space and are active only during the night.

Understanding Mice

The House Mouse in Its Natural Habitat

The common western house mouse (see color photos on pp. 10 and 45) lives almost exclusively in human dwellings, as does the Northern house mouse; in Eastern Europe and Asia, on the other hand, the common Western house mouse makes the deserts, prairies, and cultured fields its primary home. The wild house mouse burrows underground, gathers nesting materials to build its nest there, and stores food in large excavated chambers. The domesticated house mouse, able to scrounge sufficient nourishment on a regular basis because of the "easier" human environment, does not store significant amounts of food.

The wild house mouse is active mainly during the night but will come out of hiding during the daytime if it feels safe. It does not hibernate. All wild mice, no matter of which species, are extremely fast; they run, climb, and jump very well. They are good swimmers, too, but make use of this faculty only in dire emergencies, as when they are in flight.

The house mouse is a communal animal, living in family colonies with its kin. Each of these "clans" marks off its territory with odor markers of urine and droppings. Mice of any other family are chased away, but the mice within one colony care deeply for one other, constantly grooming each other's fur. Any place on its body a mouse cannot reach is licked clean by a relative. This family solidarity and unity can reach such proportions that several females might bring forth their young in the same nest, nursing the litters collectively (see "Nest Building and the Raising of Litters," page 70.) Nevertheless, a mouse colony is not always peaceful and happy. Males often fight for dominance in the social structure. The winner's rank is by no means secure for long, but is challenged again and again (see "Fighting for Rank and Territory," page 69).

In its natural habitat, the house mouse reproduces from spring to fall, mainly during the summer, when there is a large food supply. Animals "subleasing" their quarters from humans, on the other hand, never lack food; they reproduce all year round, having as many as eight litters a year with four to eight young in each litter. With such a surging increase in the number of mice, one would think that their territory would be overcrowded in no time. Nature, however, has equipped mice with an effective means of birth control. Whenever the mouse population grows too large, many young females become less fertile; the reduced fertility is caused by a delay in heat (ovulation periods). This natural birth control is, in fact, a result of hormonal changes caused by the stress of overcrowded conditions.

This "emergency brake" phenomenon is rare in a natural environment; the mice's predators usually prevent such population explosions. Mice are constantly threatened by cats and their wild relatives, by various species of martens, particularly the weasel, polecat, fisher, and ferret, by foxes, hedgehogs, porcupines, shrews, snakes, various daytime birds of prey, and owls. Mice are never safe from these, not at any time nor in any location. Owls noiselessly swoop down on mice during the supposedly safe cover of the night; shrews and weasels even follow them to their nests and hiding places.

Mass reproduction is possible only when mice escape notice while they are nesting in storage facilities. The animals will almost always find a way to stored food supplies, building their nests in the most inaccessible places. Even though mice are seed and grain eaters by nature, almost no human food is safe from them.

The wild house mouse of today is still considered a pest. The problem is not really what these rodents eat; it is more a question of contamination by mouse urine and droppings. Wild house mice can be a danger to humans as carriers of diseases, since they come into contact with the filthiest places to be found. No wonder the wild house mouse is an extremely unwelcome guest in homes, sheds, and supply rooms.

Concise Mouse Anatomy

The house mouse is a rodent with head-body length of 3 to 4 inches (7.5–10.2 centimeters). Its tail is between 2⅞ and 4 inches (7.2–10.2 centimeters) long, is practically hairless, and has 150 to 200 scaly rings. Mice weigh anywhere from ⅖ to 1 ounce (12–28 grams). The fur color is a uniform lead gray or "mouse" gray, slightly lighter on the animal's belly. The fur is short and snug; the ears are large and almost hairless.

One of the identifying characteristics of the house mouse is a prominent, sharp-edged protrusion on the back of the incisors, clearly distinguishing the house mouse from the otherwise similar wood mouse and yellow-necked mouse. Both of the latter species are considerably browner in color and have lighter bellies; even their tails are darker on top, lighter on the bottom, but they are still easily confused with house mice.

The house mouse and other members of the genus *Mus* each has 16 teeth arranged according to the following dental formula:

$$\frac{1.0.0.3. \; = \; \text{upper jaw}}{1.0.0.3. \; = \; \text{lower jaw}} \times 2 = 16 \text{ teeth}$$

According to this formula, both sides of the upper as well as lower jaws of the house mouse contain the following teeth (from front to back): one incisor (1), no canine tooth (0), no bicuspids (0), and 3 molars (3) (see illustration below and on page 44).

All other mice (of the genus *Mus*), rats (of the genus *Rattus*), and even hamsters

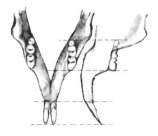

Like all rodents, the house mouse has continuously growing incisors without any roots.

(golden hamsters as well as dwarf hamsters) have the same dental formula, and thus the same dental structure as the house mouse. There are other characteristics common to house mice and other long-tailed mice: a pointed nose and a split upper lip. The forefeet of a house mouse have 4 toes each, the hind feet have five toes each.

A house mouse's appendix contains large numbers of bacteria for the twofold purpose of breaking down indigestible foods and producing B-complex vitamins, in particular Vitamin B 1.

The mouse takes the light and soft excrement produced by the appendix direct from its anal region and eats it. These are the famous "appendix pills" containing the vital vitamin B. For that reason, it would be wrong to prevent mice from eating some of their droppings.

The house mouse has a normal body temperature of 100.4°F to 102.2°F (38°–39° C), a temperature of 107.6°F (42°C) being fatal. Mice can easily develop this high temperature in an enclosed container (aquarium, terrarium) subjected to direct sunlight.

House Mouse Behavior

The house mouse is a small, defenseless rodent that has learned to hide. While scurrying about in its territory, it tries to stay under cover at all times. In unknown territory, it runs for only short distances at a time, constantly stopping dead in its tracks, waiting without moving a muscle.

If at all possible, a mouse keeps to the darker areas of its territory (the cage, too, is its territory); it just does not relish much light. A wild house mouse stays in hiding for most of the day; a caged pet mouse spends much time in its nest during daytime hours. If you have provided a sleep or nest house, the mouse builds its nest there, using it not only as a refuge but also as a storage chamber for the choicest tidbits. In many cases, several mice share a nest and build a second one for rearing their young. While all members of a colony have access to the common nest, no member of another mouse colony is allowed into the nursery.

Recent research has shown that mice are capable of falling into a state of numb rigidity in case of freezing temperatures or scarcity of food, thereby preventing freezing or starving to death.

Social Behavior

The house mouse lives in a "clan" colony structure (see "The House Mouse in Its Natural Habitat," **page 66**), ruled by a

Mice are extremely clean animals, never tiring of the joy of grooming themselves.

strict social order that ensures that all kin live together in relative harmony. The advantages of community living are obvious; a colony or pack offers better protection against enemies or intruders; it is easier to find and explore more hiding places and passages leading to them; it is usually easier to obtain larger food supplies. Pooled efforts in raising the young, warmer nests, and mutual grooming also play an important role. Naturally, a mouse is able to live just with its immediate family, but given time and favorable conditions, this little family will soon become a many-membered clan.

Fighting for Rank and Territory

Each colony is headed by a particularly strong or "shrewd" buck, the "lead buck," who has the right of mating with all females in heat. In their subordinate rank in the social structure, the other males are excluded from mating both because the females reject them and because the dominant leader prohibits them.

However, these low-ranked mice by no means accept their subordinate role forever; they challenge the position of the dominant male by constantly picking a fight. Such fights begin by a mouse drumming its tail on the ground and stamping with its hind feet (see "Body Language," page 72); the combatants then bite each other. The animals might stop fighting for a while, but keep threatening each other in this manner. If one of them, certain of defeat, wants to stop the fight, it makes a squeaking noise. It may even strike a pose signifying humilia-

During a fight, the males beat at each other with their forepaws.

tion by standing on its hind legs and pressing the forefeet against its body. At this, the antagonist stops its attacks, and the fight is over. However, these same animals can be involved in a new fight at any time.

Should the dominant male succumb in such a fight, all males of the community will bite him. This tells him that, as of now, he is in last place in the social order. Since this male is usually an older animal, he has to give up his place for a younger

Biting is very common in fights for dominance. Injuries are seldom fatal, however, since the winner immediately accepts the display of humility on the part of the defeated animal.

relative. The strongest one of them will become the new master of the community.

Should you add a new buck to your mouse community, he will be attacked and bitten by all resident males. Since the mouse cannot run away, and since it finds itself in a foreign territory, it is totally intimidated and won't offer any resistance against the biting attacks. Most of the time, it will be dead in a matter of hours, or after one day. It is not the bites that kill; those bites, in fact, are rather harmless; it is the stress of being alone and totally helpless against these attacks in a territory not its own. In addition, the mice of the colony menace the intruder with high piercing shrieks in the ultrasonic range (see "Sound Language," **page 72**). In a natural environment, the buck would never have dared to enter the territory of the strange colony; the odor markers would have shown him the territorial borders. He would have run back to his own territory as soon as he realized he was crossing a border or as soon as he encountered the threats of a strange mouse community. There are mice colonies where the females are involved in similar fights for dominance.

Nest Building and the Raising of Litters

In families whose females live together in harmony the practice of building community nests is much more common than in the rare families with cantankerous females. In these common nests, several females share the duties of raising all of the young. It can even happen that all young are nursed by all mothers. One of the reasons for these community nests might be the warmth they provide, new litters needing a nest temperature of approximately 86°F (30°C) to thrive.

The amount of building material for these common nests depends on the temperature of the nest location and on the number of its inhabitants. The more inhabitants, the thinner the nest walls, since the animals provide each other with body heat. Should the temperature rise above 86°F, any further nest improvements stop; should it drop to about 50°F (10°C), the nest is built strong and compact. At even lower temperatures, the mice do not feel comfortable anymore and try to move to a better place, preferring the darkest and warmest corner they can find.

If a young animal falls out of the nest or leaves it too early to go exploring, the mother picks it up and returns it. Sometimes a mother will move her whole litter into a new nest. For these relocations, the young take a certain body position: They

When a young one prematurely leaves the nest, the mother brings it back immediately, carrying it at the nape of the neck.

roll up, legs and tail pressed to the body, almost forming a ball. It is a convenient transport position; the mother can carry the young without their spread-eagled legs and tail being caught on any obstacles. The young one will maintain this "carrying rigidity" as long as the mother holds on to it, a reflex that becomes extremely important when mother and young are fleeing from an enemy. It takes the baby a few seconds after being put down to "wake up," stretch, and be limber again.

When fleeing, a mouse is capable of speeds up to 7½ miles per hour (12 kilometers per hour) over short distances. These speeds, impressive for such small animals, have been measured particularly for females carrying a young one.

Following the death of a female, other does with litters of the same age will often accept the orphans. However, it also happens that a doe will kill infants not her own. Maybe the orphaned young lose the typical colony odor, or maybe they are making sounds in an ultrasonic range that enrage other females.

It is astonishing that house mice will even nurse babies of different species. Researchers have placed not only the young of yellow-necked mice and wood mice underneath house mice, but also those of field mice, desert jerboas and shrews, and they **were all accepted without hesitation.**

Mice are devoted parents. Wild house mouse females defend their young even against cats, dogs, and people by covering the young with their bodies and trying to bite the attacker. Usually, this will mean the end of the mother, but she would never

Mice can show a lot of courage, particularly when they are trying to protect their young. In such a situation, they may even confront a cat and threaten it.

dream of running away. Even totally tame females may suddenly become furies, jump up, and bite your finger if you come too close to the litter in her nest. The males do not take care of the nestlings. However, they protect females as well as young from any intruding mice from other communities.

Odor Language

Mice have a highly developed odor language, and they cope with their environment mainly by smell. Recognition of enemy as well as kin is totally "nose-oriented." Within the realm of mice, community members and strangers are recognized by their odor; mice can even distinguish between individuals.

Odor language "talks" in many different ways. There are the urine markers directing community members to promising food supplies, to the nest, and to escape routes. The markers left by glands in the soles of the animal's feet are important orientation signals. These glands are arranged in such

Understanding Mice

a way that their secretions tell other mice not just who walked by, but the time and direction of transit. Finally, the females let the males know when they are ready to mate by emitting an inviting odor.

Sound Language

People can pick up only faint squeaking noises that the mice use only on rare occasions (in fights and in arguments about a particularly choise morsel of food). Young mice call in high-pitched voices when they have crawled out of the nest or have been dragged out hanging onto their mother's nipples.

Considering that mice are very sociable animals living together in a community, these squeaks would be an extremely limited sound language. We have discovered recently that mice actually have much more to say to each other, but they are "talking" in a pitch not discernible by the human ear; mice communicate on a supersonic level. We believe that their chirping and peeping in this high frequency is intensive and varied. These sounds can be recorded by an instrument called an oscillograph, and the sounds are interpreted by behavior studies. However, without complicated technical aids, people have no access to this world of ultrasound communication, and therefore no access to the sound language of mice.

Body Language

Even though the orientation of mice is based primarily on odor signals, and even though ultrasound communication seems to be much more significant than we had formerly assumed, mice have an additional communication faculty: body language.

In any meeting between two mice of the same colony, the animals turn towards each other, first front, then back, to take an odor "reading." One mouse tells another very clearly that it would like to be groomed in a certain place by pointing that body part towards its kin. Occasionally, a mouse might throw itself to the ground and turn over, inviting another to lick its stomach. Usually, however, it turns chin, face, the top of the head, and the ears towards a friend for licking and cleaning.

Then, there are certain threatening gestures: firmly planted, tense legs, nose held up high, beating of the tail. A mouse raises every hair of its fur, uses its tail as a drum, and stamps its hind feet on the ground. The front paws are used for a stamping on an adversary (see illustration on **page 69**).

Finally, there are the poses acknowledging defeat. In a fight for dominance, a defeated animal uses body language to tell

This defensive pose is intended to chase away an enemy; at the same time, it is a signal indicating that the mouse is ready and willing to fight.

Understanding Mice

A mouse that has been defeated in a fight shows submission by standing on its hind legs, pressing the front paws against its body, and presenting its unprotected throat to the winner.

the winner it is giving up; it sits up like a begging dog, leans its head way back, and presses its front paws against its body— clearly a pose of humiliation.

The Senses

Vision

The house mouse cannot see very well. Because of the position of the eyes on the side of the head and the eyes' highly convex shape, the mouse is incapable of detailed vision. The mouse relies instead on its superb sense of smell (see page 74) and a well-developed sense of touch (see page 74).

Precisely because of its bulging, semispherical "button eyes," however, the mouse has an almost perfect visual field, enabling it to see an enemy approach from any direction. Mice can discern movement much better than stationary objects. Cats have clearly recognized this; they wait in front of a mouse hole without moving a muscle.

While golden hamsters are totally color blind, and guinea pigs are capable of distinguishing between blue, green, yellow, and red, mice are believed to perceive the colors yellow and red.

Hearing

The house mouse has a well-developed sense of hearing; it is particularly well equipped to discern sounds of high frequency ranges. Many of the sounds made by mice exceed the human audiofrequency range of 16,000–20,000. This means that humans cannot hear mouse sounds, while mice can. The threshold of hearing for

Mice have a highly developed sense of touch. Their sensitive vibrissae (tactile hairs or whiskers), pointing in all directions, are equipped with extremely fine nerves. With their help, a mouse can judge whether it will be able to squeeze through a particular hole.

mice is approximately 100,000 Hz (see "Sound Language," page 72).

You can deduce the excellence of a mouse's hearing by the silence of its enemies. All natural enemies of mice hunt their prey without making a sound. Cats have soft paws for soundless movement; the plumage and wings of flying owls make no noise that could warn a mouse and cause it to seek cover in time. Because these predators are inaudible, mice fall prey to their enemies frequently.

Their relatively large external ears are another indication that mice have a good sense of hearing. Compared to house mice, voles living mainly underground have tiny ears and an inferior sense of hearing. The structure of the inner ear of a mouse is much more complicated than even that of the human ear. The mouse's middle ear has the same three sound-transmitting bones, but the cochlea, the spiral-shaped part of the inner ear, has three spirals, the human cochlea having only one.

Smell

Of all senses, a mouse's sense of smell is by far the most developed. Mice use their nose for "nosing out" food, identifying friend or foe, tracking down a mating partner, finding their way around a burrow. For this last purpose, they construct regular odor trails (see "Odor Language," page 71); without these trails, they would run around aimlessly. They even recognize you, their keeper, only by the way you smell. Even though mice do not get emotionally attached, they'll let you know whether they like you or "can't stand your smell."

To develop such a remarkably powerful sense of smell, the interior of the nose had to become a prodigious smelling organ. For an animal as small as a mouse, its mucous membrane is huge, and equipped with many very fine nerve endings. Even portions of the conchae, the shell-like projections in the nose, hairless and always a little wet, are provided with numerous olfactory nerves.

Touch

As regular "night owls," preferring dark places even during the day, mice have a well-developed sense of touch. Large and strong vibrissae, i.e., tactile hairs or whiskers, are arranged all around their mouths, the roots surrounded by a net of highly sensitive tactile nerves (just like a cat's whiskers). These whiskers do not point just to the side; some point downward; a few are even arranged above the eyes, pointing straight up. Mice have additional tactile hairs at the outside of their legs and on the sides of their bodies. Aided by these whiskers, a mouse can determine in a split second whether it will fit into a particular hiding place or hole.

Additional Source of Information

American Fancy Rat and Mouse Association
9230 64th Street
Riverside, California 92509

National Mouse Club (N. M. C.)
c/o Honorable Secretary
26 Grasmere Road
Bradford 2, Yorkshire, England

Index

Index

Index

Index

Perfect for Pet Owners!